Don't Be Afraid
to Say You're Lonely

Christopher Martin was ordained a few
years ago after a long spell as Religious
Broadcasting Officer of the Independent
Broadcasting Authority, where he did
much to foster social action broadcasting,
both on local radio and on television. He is
Resident Chaplain at the Royal Star &
Garter Home for disabled ex-servicemen,
and earns his living by his word processor.
Amongst his more recent books are *Trespass
Against Francis* and *One God – Three Gods?*,
both written to go with HTV networked
religious television series on which he
worked. He is currently engaged on a
similar project on "Pilgrimage".

CHRISTOPHER MARTIN

Don't Be Afraid to Say You're Lonely

Collins
FOUNT PAPERBACKS

First published in Great Britain by
Fount Paperbacks, London in 1987

Copyright © Christopher Martin 1987

Made and printed in Great Britain by
William Collins Sons & Co Ltd, Glasgow

for J.L.A.

without whom this would have been more heartfelt
and finished sooner

Contents

Introduction

The Word
A pen appeared, and the god said:
"Write what it is to be
Man." And my hand hovered
long over the bare page

until there, like footprints
of the lost traveller, letters
took shape on the page's
blankness, and I spelled out

the word "lonely". And my hand moved
to erase it: but the voices
of all those waiting at life's
window cried out loud: "It is true."

Anon

Perhaps you have never felt lonely. Maybe you are one of those who can put their hand on their heart and say "Never". Then this book is not for you, and be thankful that it isn't. You must be one of those people whose lives are full and busy and interesting, and for whom there is never a dull moment. Yes, of course, you are on your own sometimes, but that is not the same thing. We all need to be alone from time to time. It would be unbearable if life were one long nonstop party and we could never have a moment to ourselves.

Being alone is not necessarily being lonely. It is a common experience to feel lonely in the middle of a crowd, when everybody else seems alien. It is common enough to feel lonely under your own roof, with other members of your household around you. At one time or another most of us have had a twinge of loneliness, and a very unpleasant sensation it is. Anyone who has had this sensation may find these pages have something to say to them. For here is an attempt to explore what loneliness is, as it afflicts us at any age from adolescence onwards. There are a few other books around on the subject; not very many, because it is a subject that we prefer not to discuss. Some of them take a brisk approach to the subject. Come on, they say, get to grips with yourself, shake yourself out of it and don't knuckle under. They read a bit like swimming instructions bawled over a megaphone to a non-swimmer out of his depth. If the cure for loneliness were simply to follow the instructions, none of us would need to be lonely.

Yet so many people are. Jeremy Seabrook's *Loneliness* (Temple, White 1972) is a moving set of interviews with an assortment of people, some obvious, others not, describing how they feel lonely. There are sketches of people in this book, too. Naturally their names have been changed, and their surroundings disguised, and not everything in quotation marks is an exact report of what they said at any one moment. But they are real people, and their loneliness is real.

For so many people are lonely, and dare not show it. If they do, they risk rejection and misunderstanding, and that only makes their loneliness worse. Other painful emotions we do feel freer to show. The days of the stiff upper lip have largely gone, and now we are encouraged to reveal something of the hurt we feel. In any case, our body language (to use the fashionable phrase) may give us away. When we are angry, our cheeks redden and our voices rise; when we are bored, we yawn and itch and don't know where to put ourselves. There is a catalogue of physical expressions that any careful observer can detect: fear, misery and sheer pain all give themselves away.

Usually these are surface emotions, that come and go. They may well be related to loneliness, but that lies deeper and usually lasts much longer, and so we take care to hide it. The Victorians could not talk about sex. A more recent generation, numbed by the slaughter of the Somme, and with no common religious convictions left, could not bear to discuss death. For us sex is quite easy to talk about, and in recent years we have begun to learn to talk about death again, and to admit our grief. What we cannot admit is loneliness.

So loneliness digs under our skin, into the core of our being. It is no respecter of persons. Anybody can be lonely, old or young, rich or poor. It is no respecter of ability, IQ, class or any of the other measures by which we pass social judgements. It can afflict and conquer the cleverest professor just as ruthlessly as it dominates the obvious misfit.

There may be no brisk cures for it, but at least by considering what it is like, as it strikes different sorts of people at different times in their lives, it need no longer be quite such an unnamable terror. For by being ready to admit to our loneliness, and recognize that other people suffer from similar symptoms, we can begin to treat it as less of a terrifying demon.

Lonely people who are Christians, or who hold some other deep religious faith, may be particularly ashamed of admitting their loneliness. They feel that they should know better, and that the relationship to God through Christ, which they claim as their own, ought to immunize them against feeling lonely. For them to admit that they are lonely sounds like admitting that their faith is all a sham. It does not follow. The Christian faith does not promise its followers a constant balm of comfort, and many of the saints have plumbed the depths of loneliness during the course of their lives.

What these pages suggest is that we should not be afraid to admit that we are lonely. It is not a matter of going round telling every stranger we meet. It may be a matter for confiding to a few close friends. Essentially it is a matter for admitting to ourselves. Once we can admit our own loneliness, we can begin to make friends with it, and so reach that much further towards the roots of what we each have it in us to become. To admit our own loneliness is an essential part of maturing as a human being.

At this point any reader who feels that they want to find out what loneliness is may prefer to go on to the next chapter. But what immediately follows has its place here, and anyone who does not read it now may be glad to come back to it afterwards.

*   *   *

This book is written to mark the twenty-first anniversary of the Carr-Gomm Society, whose business is to provide homes for lonely people. It now houses over eight hundred people, in small "families" nearly half in London and the rest right across England, from Plymouth to Tyneside. The only qualification required of those who live in them is that they are lonely. Less than one in ten of them have walked straight in from the outside world and said, "I am lonely, please may I live with you". Most of the rest of them have been elsewhere on the way. About one in four of them have had a history of psychiatric illness.

Many new residents arrive via the Department of Health and Social Security's resettlement service, the probation service, and local authority housing and social services department. For as Tim Osborne-Jones, the Director of the society from 1977 to 1986, likes to point out, few of the residents of its homes are "only lonely". By the time that they come to live in one of the houses, their loneliness has complications, mental illness, some sort of police record, or an evident inability to live on their own.

The Carr-Gomm Society can justly claim to have been a pioneer in this particular field. Given continuing government support for several decades now, housing associations have become an accepted part of our social landscape. Whether established as charitable ventures, or as co-operative undertakings, they have expanded to provide something like ten per cent of the nation's homes. Out of that large number, the Carr-Gomm Society's tally of a hundred homes does not sound very many. Yet it stands as a pioneering venture because of the way that it has identified its clientele. To live in a Carr-Gomm house is to admit to having been lonely.

The Carr-Gomm Society owes its name to its founder, Richard Carr-Gomm, OBE. Now in his mid-sixties, he is the third of four brothers who grew up unostentatiously in an upper-middle-class home between the wars: with a governess, for instance, but no motor car. There was a family pew in church, which they all filled every Sunday morning. Originally plain Carrs, they owed their double-barrelled name to a settlement by a maiden great-great aunt, Miss Gomm, which carried with it estates of working-class terraced housing in Bermondsey and Rotherhithe.

Richard, the delicate one of the family, went to the recently founded public school of Stowe, and was about to follow his brothers to Oriel College, Oxford, when war broke out. He at once volunteered, and in due course was commissioned into the Coldstream Guards. His war service took him to Normandy, and he still bears the scar of a shell-wound that he suffered when he poked his head out of his tank in the course of a battle. He recovered sufficiently from it to be back on the Rhine in 1945, and by that time had decided to make soldiering his career.

So he soldiered around the Middle East for several years. In 1953 he decided to use his leave to make his way home overland from Sicily, living rough. In his privately published autobiography, *Push On the Door*, he describes how he felt then:

> During my travels I was often lonely. Away from my family (except for leave) since the beginning of the war, I had been a member of a set of six or so brother officers who were friends, and we generally made up parties between us. I had enjoyed the relationship of all ranks inside the army which had come from shared work, hardship and boredom. On this journey I had neither family nor friends. I am better at getting on with groups than with individuals but here I had neither and missed them both.

He then had a London posting, and as Captain of the Buckingham Palace Guard could entertain whom he wished, thus meeting Dr Billy Graham, over for his early Harringay missions in 1954 and 1955. Richard Carr-Gomm put to the evangelist his growing desire to do something more worthwhile with his life. Dr Graham urged him to continue soldiering. He ignored the advice, resigned his commission, turned down the chance to go as ADC to the Kabaka of Buganda, and went to offer his services as a home help in Bermondsey, where the family estates were.

As a char, he soon found lonely old people, and thought how much happier they would be if they could share a home, and had the vision of lonely people of all ages forming households together. So with £450 from his gratuity he bought 30 Eugenia Road, and from that beginning came the Abbeyfield Society, with its houses for elderly people up and down the country. But the society dropped its pilot. By now married to Susan Gibbs, and starting a family, Richard had two spells in Uganda. It was not until 1964, by then employed as a librarian in Bermondsey, that he started again, this time determined to keep his ideal of mixing ages, and so came the Carr-Gomm Society.

The society is a charitable housing association, and now has over a hundred homes up and down England, from Tyneside to Plymouth, with altogether about eight hundred residents. So there is an average of eight people in every home, most with its resident housekeeper. The society's headquarters are in two adjoining terraced houses in Gomm Road, Bermondsey, and around the country its homes are ordinary places in ordinary streets; or even flats – certainly not mansions behind laurel bushes.

Richard Carr-Gomm's vision was to create under each roof a family. While rules are few, and should be agreed by all the residents, all the members of each house are encouraged to meet together once a week, and talk out their common interests and concerns. Not everybody wants to come; some will have nothing to say. A newcomer may be sitting warily, with an unread magazine open, in one corner. In a good house, with a good spirit, newcomers cannot stay long in their shells. Somebody may have the record-player on a bit too loud ("Oh, turn it down, Clarry"), somebody else may be in one of their moods, but then this is a family. The resident "granny" is knitting for the baby that one of the young women is expecting, the resident "granddad" passing on his skills as an electrician to the lad who is trying to mend a fuse. And though the signs are no longer there saying "Push on the door" a visitor is easily made to feel welcome.

Beyond that, Richard Carr-Gomm has always believed that people are naturally religious, and hoped that each house would find some way of giving formal expression to the simple faith in the goodness of God that is so much his own. Not every house finds this easy; so many people's religious sensibility has never had encouragement to grow, and so the mutual support that residents find from one another has to find less self-conscious means of expression. At least there are Christmas parties, and to go to one is to witness a great communal effort to celebrate. The streamers fly, even the most withdrawn person is coaxed into wearing a paper hat, crisps scatter on the church hall floor, and towards the end of the evening round the old joanna a sing-song engulfs the whole company; and there may even be something of a knees-up. So at least for one jolly evening, and steadily through the long days and weeks and months of the year, the Carr-Gomm Society puts its finger in the dyke against the huge tides of loneliness.

1.

What Is Loneliness?

Loneliness is the leprosy of our day. Its sufferers who ring their bells clamour for attention and at the same time warn off everyone in earshot. So most lonely people learn to muffle the sound and pretend that nothing is wrong. They know that the pathetic tinkle will drive others away and make their predicament worse. If only they can conceal the noise, then they might just pass as normal, sociable human beings. They do not seriously expect to overcome their distress, and they regard it as their own ghastly secret. What they fail to realize is how very many other people are suffering from the identical complaint. Most of us are more or less lonely, and are deeply afraid to admit it, even in a whisper to ourselves.

Ourselves includes you and me, but it is easier to think about loneliness if we pretend that we are thinking about "them". In what follows, you may perhaps notice something of yourself in "them". Don't expect to find everything. Loneliness has many forms and it afflicts different people in different ways, at different stages of their lives. But at one time or another any of us may catch a particular twinge of the ache that lies beneath it all. At least to be able to recognize the symptoms, and realize how common they are, is the door to the healing process.

For loneliness is a form of misery that stems from feeling unwanted. Only those who suffer from it can put a label on what is wrong, if they dare, and they may well not. Nobody else wants to know. For anyone to complain to even the most sympathetic listener of a feeling of loneliness is to invite rejection. It somehow makes them feel that it is at least partly their fault. Mainly their fault, even; there they are, ears bent to hear the moan, and they should be the ones able to offer an instant cure. They cannot do it. So they are left feeling guilty at their own inadequacy, and their self-protective instinct is to freeze. They may bully or bluster a bit, to hide the fact that they can take no more for the moment. The person complaining of loneliness has come to expect that, and wheedles with spaniel self-pity.

For there is a natural limit to the amount of the moan that anyone else can blot up. "Let's meet again next Tuesday", they may say, anxiously seeking to limit the encounter. Immediately the person complaining of loneliness is wary. "So you can't bear to listen" is the thought. "You too are part of the great plot to leave me trapped in my loneliness." And so the sense of rejection screws itself up another nervous notch tighter. Consequently nobody likes to admit that they are lonely. To do so only makes it worse.

It is just as bad for the listener. That sense of guilt runs deep. Could something more have been said? Or was that the wrong thing to say? In the end comes a shrug of the shoulders. To suggest another meeting next Tuesday was as much as could be done. It would be a relief, quite honestly, for that further meeting to be cancelled. Maybe the other person will cry off. It would be unkind to ditch them. Behind all that unease, the listener has a hidden fear. Perhaps loneliness is infectious. The last thing anyone wants to do is to catch it from somebody else. The hardest thing in the world is to admit to feeling lonely too.

And how would that help? If someone wants to pour out their feelings of loneliness, they are not expecting their listener to express the same feelings. How could that help? Anyone desperate enough to pour out their feelings is surely looking for reassurance and strength. It is hardly going to help them for the listener to admit to similar feelings. To do that calls for such a level of mutual trust that all the barriers of self-respect tremble.

Take Michael and James, two fellows whom life has used hard, sitting across a table from one another in the pub. Michael is in his sixties, Irish, his friend James twenty years younger, from Yorkshire. The whole discussion is about whether Michael will ring up his sister in Canada, as a start to resolving all his practical problems. The two men protest their friendship, verge on a quarrel, make it up, go round and round the question of how to find the telephone number in Ontario. Skin-deep beneath is how they admit to their common loneliness. It is easier for them to play roles, Michael as the one in need, James the organizer. Their want of one another's support and companionship is evident. They cannot find the words and gestures to express it. Even with the help of beer, they cannot quite find the trust. Two hours later, they are no nearer ringing Canada; all they can do is spiral downwards into their own wells of loneliness.

In every one of us there is something of Michael and James. Loneliness is no respecter of persons. It strikes where it will. It is as much a disease of our times as any other that achieves medical recognition. Some twenty years ago it looked as if many of the familiar scourges were on their way to being eliminated. Smallpox was under control, diphtheria and tuberculosis no longer fearful plagues, and pneumonia a fear of the past. Even the nursery ailments – whooping cough, measles and the rest – were no longer the bogeys that they had once been. At least across the developed world, it was beginning to seem as if medical science had effectively mastered the infections that had once raged unchecked. Then in our own day new dread diseases emerge: AIDS is only the most obvious plague for which there as yet seems no sure remedy.

Loneliness is another. Its germs have always been around, but there are good reasons why it has now so firmly established its grip. It is enough to sketch them out very barely, even if that means making sweeping statements. In Britain over the last generation or so, let alone what has happened elsewhere, society has let go of many of the things that provided it with a sense of community. Wartime certainly gave everybody a sense of belonging. Across the social classes family life was generally closer and more secure. Now so much of the frame that gave everyone a feeling of where they fitted in has rotted. We cling to our state occasions, such as royal weddings, to give ourselves some sense of common identity, and sport plays a part as well. But general acceptance of the law, of the Church as expressing a religion that somehow held us together, even an everyday sense of patriotism – these are all weaker than we like to think they were. Rare exceptions to that weakening make the point. The uprush of blood over the Falklands, the solidarity of mining villages during the year-long strike, stand out as recent reminders. Under pressure as a nation, or as a community under threat, we rally. There is less room for loneliness then.

Nostalgia for the good old days runs through every generation, even from the classic Egyptian text of the fifteenth century BC that complained that young people were not as well-behaved as they used to be. To blame the increase of loneliness on changing social conditions is particularly dangerous. Apart from anything else, loneliness is not well documented. If people are reluctant now to admit to being lonely, so they always have been. The only difference is that nowadays we have become more conscious of it. Even though lonely people themselves hesitate to admit it, we are beginning to learn to talk about it. It is like other developments in our time. We laugh at the Victorians for their prudishness about sex, yet talk about it endlessly. Till quite recently, we used to turn our backs on their obsession with death. It is only within the last ten years or so that we have once more begun to admit death into our conversation. The growth in the number of hospices is the most eloquent witness to our changed attitudes. Though it is still rare for anybody to die in their own bed, surrounded by relatives, at least the dying are no longer shovelled away quite so unthinkingly to do their beastly business out of sight. We are even learning once more how to let the bereaved express their grief. It is no longer a matter of stiff upper lips and carrying on as normal. We are learning once more that those who have lost somebody near and dear to them should be able to mourn, that it is a natural and human and right thing to be able to do. So little by little ghastly funeral gatherings where relatives discussed the weather give way to occasions whose legitimate host is grief.

Death indeed offers loneliness its most respectable foothold in society. The picture that we most naturally have is of an elderly person who has lost a partner after a lifetime together. For a few months somebody in that state can be sure of sympathy. We all recognize the inevitability of that loss. Anyone younger can only admire a couple whose marriage has lasted half a century or so. It is not too difficult to listen for a little while to those cries of loneliness and grief. Apart from anything else, they are not likely to be infectious.

Even so, sympathy is limited. Two sisters-in-law, both well into their seventies, lost their husbands at much the same moment. Some six months later they met again at a family occasion. "Well," said one briskly to the other, "I've done my mourning now, and it is high time you stopped." A few weeks later the brisk lady was as good as her word, and married her childhood sweetheart, himself not long widowed. Her sister-in-law was left to grieve, feeling that her grief was no longer socially approved, and that her resulting loneliness was indecent.

For outside the confines of grief, loneliness has few socially acceptable perches. The wife of a sailor, or some other man whose business takes him away from home for long spells, may be entitled to a pinch or two of sympathy for having to be on her own so much. It is only a pinch. She chose to marry him, and must have been aware what to expect. Other deserted spouses can expect less. The families of prisoners may suffer almost as much as the inmates, for the blame of the crime washes off on to them. Or anyone whose partner walks out on them invites the disapproval of neighbours. For one of them to walk out must mean that the other was unbearable to live with, and now deserves to feel lonely.

For loneliness does have much to do with the way other people treat the person who is caught on the raw. The sense of being rejected is the front door to loneliness. Slam that front door to keep out an unfriendly world, and then loneliness has nothing to do but feed on itself and grow. "Hell is other people" said Jean-Paul Sartre in his wartime play *Huis Clos* – "L'enfer c'est les autres" – and so provided those who see themselves as lonely with their defiant slogan. Or there is the Steinberg cartoon of the harassed executive saying, "I owe it to myself to have a nervous breakdown". That, too, is not far from the cry of the individuals who have discovered within themselves the secret fungus of loneliness.

But loneliness does not enjoy the cachet of a medically approved disease. When someone admits that they suffer from an illness with a long classical name, and one that leads to fearsome treatment, they arouse a measure of interest. While most of us remain frightened of madness in any form, we like to assume that it is not infectious. So we are ready to express polite concern for someone who tells us that they have been diagnosed and treated for schizophrenia or manic-depression. Those clinical terms provide a safety curtain. The poor so-and-so must have gone through a long process of medical examination and treatment to reach the point where he can tell us, almost with a show of pride, the name of his condition. He is displaying his battle-honours to us, and we can safely take a gracious interest in them. For at least we are safe from those scars.

Yet those registered mental conditions do lie somewhere beyond the no-man's land of loneliness. Even though the advertisements for mental health organizations remind us that one in five of us will spend some part of our lives as mental patients, those of us who have so far escaped that predicament may like to think that we are quite immune. We are in greater peril than we care to acknowledge. For loneliness is the broad threshold to a great deal of mental illness. The tragedy is that medical practice does not recognize loneliness as a condition that needs treatment.

Later in this book, the matter will need considering in greater detail. For the moment it is enough to make the point that in treating patients with anti-depressants and tranquillizers, general practitioners may often be failing to diagnose the problem as loneliness. Medical training does not teach them how to do so, and there are no certain remedies. Doctors might argue that their training has to do with the health of the patient's body; and if they are specialists, of their minds. They are not taught to identify loneliness as a condition which they are qualified to treat.

For to use old-fashioned language, loneliness is a condition of the soul, and conventionally the cure of souls is the business of ministers of religion, not of medical practitioners. "Soul" does sound an old-fashioned word, and it is worth considering why, and what we are to say instead if we cannot bring ourselves to use it. "Soul" sounds old-fashioned because it no longer seems to have a function. We appear to be able to say all we need to about ourselves without using the word. It seems a bit like an appendix, something we have outgrown and for which we have no longer any practical use.

Or "soul" sounds like "ether". Nineteenth-century physicists, who were trying to understand how light waves travelled, conceived this notion of ether – a gas too rarefied to detect with scientific instruments, but which must be everywhere – to explain how light travels.

"Soul" seems as out of date as "ether" because we now know so much more than we did about the nature of the universe and the way that human beings function. In particular the advances of psychology over the last hundred years have given us a far greater understanding of the workings of our minds, and psychiatry has developed its own methods for understanding what is wrong, and for its treatment.

Should we then think of loneliness as a "personality disorder" and refer all those who are suspected of suffering from it to a psychiatrist? That is what often happens. A busy GP may keep a patient going on Valium, to guard against depression, or on some mild barbiturate drug. But when the patient continues to come to the surgery, and these doses have lost their effect, the next step is a referral to a psychiatrist. For by then the sufferer has crossed the steppes of loneliness and is somewhere on the other side in the tracts of mental illness.

For there is a clear connection between loneliness and mental illness. Tim Osborne-Jones, until 1986 Director of the Carr-Gomm Society, has observed that amongst those who come to live in the Society's homes, there are very few who are "only lonely". Many of those presenting themselves have some history of mental illness, and something like a quarter of them have had spells in mental hospital.

Loneliness may then develop into a "personality disorder" a condition calling for psychiatric treatment. But it is not just that. It is a condition from which any one of us may suffer, more or less painfully, at least for short spells. To feel lonely is as natural as to feel any other emotion – fear, joy, anger or whatever. It is a condition of the human spirit (allowing that "spirit" may seem an easier word to handle than "soul"). It is natural and it is normal. The difference is that we are afraid to say that we are suffering from it. We are encouraged to display our other emotions. It is nowadays generally accepted as healthy that we do express our anger, our fear and our delight. Who now sees virtue in passing through life without a flicker of emotion? Yet we have this great inhibition in expressing our feelings of loneliness. As a result, they get buried inside us and fester, and we may well end up on the psychiatrist's couch.

As a nation, we should save ourselves a great deal of money and misery if GPs were ready to identify a patient's complaint as loneliness. It is not enough to try to suppress it with drugs. Drugs may keep patients ticking over for a long time, but they do not tackle the root of the problem. So often the problem is that the patient feels rejected by those around him, and is in consequence lonely.

Obviously the people most likely to feel lonely are those who live alone, as something like four million adults now do. To be alone is not necessarily to be lonely. Many people are content to live by themselves, may even have made a deliberate choice to do so. Others stumble into living alone, through bereavement, through the break-up of a marriage or other partnership. To live alone after living with other people is to confront loneliness head on. There is nobody at home to talk to, and it is very quiet. At first the place may not even feel like home, just a pad. For such individuals, Deanna Maclaren's *The Single File* (Sphere 1983) brims with practical advice, and has a long and sensible chapter about how to combat the sense of loneliness.

Yet any one person's experience of loneliness may well not match another's. Henry is a man approaching forty. Some ten years ago he was divorced, and the mother had custody of their two children. When she died of cancer, the children were left in the care of her parents. Then Henry, having been a successful businessman, found himself made redundant.

He went on the dole, and moved from bedsit to bedsit. One day he took an overdose, but someone found him, and the next thing he knew was that he was in an ambulance on his way to hospital, where they succeeded in pumping him out. A year later, still on his own, he is beginning to come to terms with himself. "I am beginning to find out who I am" he says, quite simply.

It is a remark that leads to the heart of the question "what is loneliness?" For each of us, the whole business of living is an attempt to answer that question. It is hard to believe that in this life there can be any fixed and final answer, for in so many ways we change as we blunder our way down the years. Yet it is still a good question. We enter life alone, and we go from it alone. In between, the business of living has mostly to do with our dealings with other people. If we are busy enough, we seem scarcely to have time to be solitary. It is a constant temptation to shy away from the question "Who am I?" by keeping busy, with our engagement books full, and even when there is no one else around, turn on the television or the radio or the record-player to keep that question at bay.

Sooner or later comes the time when we are on our own. We may fall ill, we may simply be stuck in the Underground, one member of a squash of secret people. We may find ourselves alone there every bit as much as we can when there is nobody else in sight. It can be at moments like these when the question "Who am I?" looms at us. To be able to examine it is the first step towards making friends with the loneliness that each one of us harbours.

The brisk approach to the sense of loneliness is to fight it. Be positive, we are urged. When the lonely person complains that he finds that difficult to do, the schoolmarm voice can only say "Try harder – be positive". It is like a bad swimming lesson: push your arms harder, kick out with your legs. Somebody frightened of water thrashes away, more certain than ever of going under. So it is with brisk advice on combating the sense of loneliness. The more that anyone follows bossy encouragement to get out and embrace life, the more its terrors appal. Loneliness becomes a secret drug, and the frightened person clings to it like a precious shadow.

A good swimming instructor encourages his pupil to feel at home in the water. "Let yourself go into it, trust it, and it will support you." That is so hard to believe. Our earliest experience of water is that we may sink in it, swallow it, perhaps even drown. How can it possibly keep us afloat? Yet it does. So long as we have breath in our lungs, we can float on it. The sea in particular, with all its salt, is naturally buoyant. As Sydney Carter observed of the Dead Sea, "You need faith to sink in this place!"

So it is with loneliness, which is as common as the air we breathe, and the water that lies all around us. Those who have successfully come to terms with being lonely are the ones who have faced the beast. When Androcles met the lion in the arena he was naturally afraid. As soon as he recognized the creature, and the creature recognized him, his fear vanished. Loneliness is only a destructive beast if we display our fear of it. Be ready to embrace it, thorns and all, and its terror begins to go.

The terror lurks under the surface. In considering our own sense of loneliness, what we are much more likely to feel at first is a sense of resentment. Life, we mutter to ourselves, was not meant to be like this. Ever since nursery school we have been coaxed into being sociable, getting on with other people, even making friends, as part of our experience of life. If we were able to start life with any confidence in ourselves, we learned without thinking to expect the world to respond. We said our friendly hello to the world, and expected it to return our greeting.

When it turns its face from us, we are hurt. We did not expect to be cold-shouldered, and it is not fair. Everybody else seems to be getting on quite cheerfully together. What is so unattractive about us that they all seem to be engaged in a conspiracy to shut us out? We have made our effort, and what more can we be expected to do? Nothing we do seems to melt the surrounding ice.

A very lonely middle-aged man goes regularly to a local day centre. He is an intelligent man, who looks back wistfully on his successful life in business and his happy home with his wife and children. He finds consolation in writing little homilies on how to combat loneliness. "You hug your dog, so don't forget to hug your child." They are brave enough words. Anybody who meets him soon discovers how locked into his own loneliness he is, and feels his resentment against a world that has slammed the door in his face. He can type these well-phrased snippets of advice, but cannot discover how to act upon them himself.

For we did not expect to be lonely. "It is not good for man to be alone" said the Lord God in the Garden of Eden, and from Adam's rib created Eve. It is in our nature to expect companionship. We may then make the discovery, as so many people do, that living in a household with other people is no guarantee against loneliness. Even within a family it is quite possible to feel lonely. Quite apart from married couples who fall apart, each prey to a private loneliness, other members of a family are liable to feel lonely: the unwanted older relation, kept at bay from the mainstream of family life; the unmarried brother or sister, the son or daughter who has always been the odd one out.

To live with other people, one's own relations or not, is no guarantee against loneliness. Under the common roof, it is still possible for one individual, or more, to grow shut in on themselves. Communication dwindles, resentment builds into misery, and loneliness has taken hold. Particularly when the past holds memories of happy togetherness taken for granted, loneliness can pounce. Till now there has hardly been need to face the question "Who am I?" It has been hidden under the frail assumption that we know who we are. Suddenly to discover that we no longer know, and that it is scarcely possible any longer to talk of "we" at all, is to come slap up against the bitterness of isolation.

Yet living with other people does reduce the risk of loneliness. Especially when people live together with some sense of common purpose, there is less room for it. A shared discipline fosters a sense of comradeship, and that is why so many unsoldierly people look back on their time in the forces with strange warmth. Sailors, and other groups of people hazarding their lives together against the elements, develop a sense of mutual dependence which leaves little space for loneliness. So people have often tried to create small communities, inspired by a certain vision of how they should live together, in the belief that they will be so fired by their common ideal that they will have no space for loneliness.

Religious communities are the most obvious example. Yet it is a mistake to suppose that they naturally display such closeness that nobody feels lonely. On the contrary, in traditional religious communities loneliness and all the devils of despair and dismay have plenty of room for manoeuvre. For such disciplined groups of dedicated men or women (or both) in their rules admit the need to leave each member a great deal of privacy in which to work out his own salvation. Closeness there may be, and a very great sense of mutual support and encouragement; but within the walls of a religious house intimacy is suspect. For any one member to become deeply committed to another goes against the tenor of the body. Members of religious communities therefore look constantly into the mirror of their own potential loneliness; but because they look through it towards a God who is other than themselves, they have some protection from its grip. Mature members of religious communities have therefore learned a lot about themselves and about their own exposure to the risk of loneliness. Not all of them easily display the gift of absorbing the loneliness that can cloud those who live their lives in the everyday world. So for a visitor to spend a few days in a religious house may be a very lonely experience; its chief comfort comes from the knowledge that the largely uncommunicative robed figures around have weathered the same pain far more intensely.

For they have spent so much time in silence, so much time essentially on their own. That is something which everybody needs to do, if they are to reach their natural maturity. Nobody is more pathetic than the person who cannot bear to be alone. At every stage of life, some spells of time on one's own are a part of the natural rhythm. For a child, those hours of private play, making and making believe, help the process of becoming at home in the world. For an adolescent, time alone, under the open sky, provides essential space for finding how to ask the deep questions. Young adults, as they pair off and start making new homes, certainly need moments on their own and away from one another. A true sign of maturity is to be content with one's own company. Growing older, with the prospect of death looming, cries out for time to oneself. Old age and decrepitude bring solitude in plenty; for those who have spent a lifetime learning not to be afraid to admit that they are lonely, the cruel burdens of old age may be somewhat easier to bear than they are for those who have scurried through life unreflectively, never expecting that this would happen to them.

Loneliness does not only happen to them. It happens to us, you and me. Until a generation ago, nobody had recognized how wide-spread loneliness was, or devised any means of support for those suffering most acutely from it. Now various national and local voluntary organizations have come into being to provide just such support. The Carr-Gomm Society is something of a pioneer, since it makes no secret of loneliness as the root problem of those it aims to help. Some dozen years earlier the Rev. Chad Varah had started the Samaritans, the telephone service that offers anybody in distress a number to ring and unburden themselves into the ear of a friendly listener. The success of the service, and its spread through the country, shows that it meets a real need. Radio phone-ins tap something of the same need, and the off-air counselling service begun by Capital Radio in its early days has found many imitators. Granada Television has developed its own form of "air-care" seeking to put viewers in touch with the appropriate social agency in their own neighbourhood.

Other organizations tackle loneliness as a side-effect of mental illness. The Richmond Fellowship, founded in 1959 by a young Dutch nurse, Elly Jansen, and still run by her, now has some hundred homes up and down the country for those coming out of psychiatric hospitals and needing somewhere to live while they find their feet. The hostels that MIND runs are for people with a history of mental illness who go out to earn their livings. There are local charitable ventures meeting a similar need, such as the Vineyard Project in Richmond, Surrey, where the crypt of a church building serves as a day centre for lonely people.

These pockets of provision, both for those in special need as well as those whose need is harder to define, touch only a small number of those who suffer from loneliness. All sorts of other activities come near the edge of it, from day centres for the elderly to youth clubs. In between adult education classes provide people with the opportunity to learn something and, more importantly, one evening a week when they can be sure of sympathetic company. One in four Londoners, we are told, for instance, enrol in an evening class. Their motives may well be mixed. In joining a class they may be making a move to combat their loneliness, even if they scarcely admit it. For how many people can put their hands on their hearts and say that they are never lonely?

2.

So Young and So Lonely

Ask a child about feeling lonely, and the question will seem strange. Jonathan is eleven, just about to go to secondary school. Trying to be helpful, he chats away about himself. Yes, he is quite often on his own, sometimes he feels bored, but then there is always the telly, and Mum will be home soon. He remembers times when he has been frightened. There was that moment when he was climbing with his Dad on Snowdon, and lost his grip, and began slithering down in the snow. That was frightening! But lonely? He knows perfectly well what the word means. But it means nothing in his own experience.

Jonathan's mother Sheila is a Youth Officer in a cathedral city in the south of England. Year by year two or three hundred young people drift through her hands. "You would expect them to be from somewhere near the bottom of the social scale", she says. "Not a bit. Most of them are middle class, several very definitely upper middle class. Oh, yes, the girls as much as the boys – rather more girls than boys, in fact."

These are youngsters who have moved away from home. Home may well be a one-parent room of some sort; it can equally well be a des. res. with Mum and Dad and all mod. con. Sheila's main job is to find them somewhere to live. The lucky ones are already in squats, and since Sheila is employed by the county, she can fight local council moves to evict them. "Otherwise, where are they to go? On supp. ben. they cannot afford b. & b." But isn't it her job, particularly with the younger ones, to coax them back home? No, they have made

32

their break, and while other people may be paid to get them back under parental care, that is not her business.

Some of them will go back home of their own accord. Girls who have had a row with Mum want to prove that they can manage on their own. After six weeks most of them have had enough. The ones who last longer than that are not likely to go back for a long time. They are the ones Sheila is concerned about.

Then there are drugs. In her city there are a couple of places where the pushers work. The police know them, of course, and every so often there is a raid. It is a cat and mouse business. Soon enough they are back at it, and the kids are ever so vulnerable.

And, yes – so obvious when you come to think about it. Yes, these kids are all basically lonely. Never thought of that before, Sheila admits, but it does run through. So many of them, not least the posh ones, come from broken homes. If we could use loneliness as the clue to helping them tackle their problems, we might start getting somewhere.

At the age of eleven, Jonathan simply has no experience of loneliness. Happy children meet the world with open faces. Some, from bad homes, may already have deep experiences of fear and misery. Even from good homes there may be the odd child who never seems to make friends or join in whatever is going on. It is probably a mistake to think of such children as lonely. Far more likely, they are quite content with their own company, using those precious years before they are sucked into the cycle of reproduction to develop their imaginations. Like Jonathan, they might admit to other unpleasant sensations, but those are unlikely to include loneliness, since loneliness goes with doubt about who I am; and for children that has not become a brooding question.

There are some adults who look back on a lonely childhood. A friend of mine whose father died when he was six recalls feeling desperately lonely. For Dad to die when ou are just about old enough to know what death is must feel as if the whole universe had slapped you in the face. Looking back after fifty years, it is easy to say, yes, I was lonely then. Yet ask not just Jonathan but other children whether they ever feel lonely, and they are puzzled by the question. Loneliness is not something that figures naturally within a child's experience. Fright and misery they may well know about; but loneliness is to do with not being sure of themselves, and they are generally too young to have come up against that feeling.

The innocence of childhood used to be a popular notion. It goes with Millais's classic picture of "Bubbles" the pretty boy in his velvet suit and fair curls. Over the last generation we have almost lost the notion of childhood – innocent or not – since our culture now treats youngsters from the time they get their new teeth as "sub-teens". Yet for two hundred years, until about 1950, the idea of childhood as innocent had a strong grip. In letting go of it we have lost something precious. One of the more surprising sayings of Jesus is "unless you become like small children you cannot enter the kingdom of heaven". At that time there was no fashion for idolizing childhood. He was pointing to the simplicity of children. They are who they are, and as they are. The duplicity only begins to set in later, as they begin to wonder about themselves and their place in the world. Once that process starts, they are indeed liable to feel lonely, but not until then.

So in two or three years' time Jonathan may well begin to know what it is to feel lonely, as the process of growing up pushes him into wondering who he really is. Underneath that process comes the hardest business of all – learning to love ourselves. Conventional morality extracts the phrase "Love your neighbour" as the basis of how we should all behave. So we all try to be nice, looking for old ladies whom we can help across the road. Niceness does not last very long, and out of its context "Love your neighbour" is no more use than sentiment. For in context we are first required to "love the Lord your God with all your heart and with all your soul and with all your mind and with all your strength". Only after that are we to "Love your neighbour … as yourself". Learning to love ourselves is a life-time's work. The idols we pin up of how we would like to be are not ourselves. They are false gods, and worshipping them does us no good. It leaves us split in half, and then we notice the gap and it can quickly become filled with the black juice of self-pitying loneliness.

Sarah had an acutely lonely teenage. She was the younger of identical twins, and though even their parents could scarcely tell them apart, Sarah knew only too painfully that her other half, Alice, was growing into another person. As children they had been happy intimates. The process of adolescence cut into that, as Sarah found that she did not know how to grow into being herself. In her mid-teens she began to suffer very acutely from anorexia nervosa; she simply could not bear to eat. Out of instinctive sympathy, Alice went off her food too, but for Sarah that only made matters worse. Doctors, specialists, hospitals – nothing seemed able to reach inside and start her on the way to a cure. Then came an evening in hospital when she had a moment, as she puts it, of absolute horror at what she was actually doing to herself. "The image became one of reality as I looked at the painfully thin almost child-like figure silhouetted against the darkness outside. It was me!" For her to see "me" in outline there was the point at which her cure could start. Out of her depths of loneliness and misery, she had caught a glimpse of herself, and knew that there was the person whom she had to begin to learn to love.

As a youth worker, Sheila says that the key to her work in helping her clients is to encourage them to form one good friendship. Usually it is girl with girl, or boy with boy, of much the same age. It need not be. If she can get a girl and a boy to become best friends, she is content. Or it may be an older girl and a younger boy; not so often the other way round, for then sex gets in the way.

If we are to think about loneliness as it affects young people, it is worth thinking about best friends. At infant school, a child has no difficulty in naming first, second and even third best friends. Towards the end of primary school, this simple labelling changes. Then it is very good and important to have a best friend, maybe one who has been a friend for ages. Come secondary school, and things change. What matters then is to be one of the group, the gaggle, the gang. Best friends do not fit easily into that pattern, though they may be the best defence against the onset of loneliness.

For as young people grow from the sunlit world of childhood into the forests of adolescence, they discover to their horror that they are on their own. Deep friendships that through these crucial years survive all the chops and changes are rare. Girls especially expect so much of one another, and are vexed when a friend does not keep matching up to all their expectations. Boys may place less demand upon a best friend, and ride together more easily. For girls need to hold hands against the rest of the dark world. Boys depend less on touch. They may maul on the playground, or in the rugby scrum. They can watch footballers hugging the goal-scorer, and even cricketers crowding round to hold a triumphant member of the eleven. As they become teenagers, they are more concerned with belonging to the gang than with finding one best friend. For them that need may blossom in their later teens.

By then best friends look together out at the world ahead. Gazing into one another's eyes is not their preoccupation. They may not even find words to express their friendship. It is enjoyments that they share, and challenges, and underlying that is trust. They get on, feel at ease and comfortable with one another, look for each other's company, expect and find warmth and understanding. In his book *The Four Loves* C. S.

Lewis made the distinction between sexual love and friendship by suggesting that the physical element was absent from friendship. Thirty years later that distinction seems exaggerated. Friends do enjoy one another as persons, do take pleasure in one another's looks, are ready to admire one another. For Lewis friendship was a meeting of minds over a pint of beer. There spoke the Oxford don. Friendship also expresses itself in a game of tennis, climbing a mountain together, anything strenuous; and then it is the association of two people with one another, body and soul, and not just a meeting of minds.

For the essence of best friendship is a readiness to challenge the universe together. It goes with a sense that nobody else fully understands, but that does not matter because the two of us are so close. So the best best friendships last, and happy are those who years and years later keep friends with somebody to whom they were first close as adolescents. More often, at that stage, best friendships are only for a time – a year or so, a term, a matter of months. While they do go on, they have an irreplaceable value. Just at the stage when a young person is learning to question life, there is somebody else with whom to do it.

Close friendships between young people of the same age and the same sex are not the only hedge against uncertainty and loneliness. Teenagers can develop good friendships with somebody half a generation older. It may be with a teacher, a youth club leader, a neighbour, a relation, a workmate. It could be with a minister of religion – the curate who suddenly emerges as something other than a figure of authority. At bottom this is the relationship between godchild and godparent. Here for a young person is somebody else, outside the family circle, on whom it is possible to lean. Here is somebody to whom it is possible to moan that school is awful, that Mum doesn't understand.

Any young people who are able to develop a friendship of

this sort are less likely to feel that the world is one great conspiracy against themselves. The high ideal of godparents was that they should be people chosen by parents to serve as lifelong friends for their children. All too often, that ideal does not work out, as people move away from one another and find it difficult to honour their promises. As a result, the Church of England at least places less emphasis on the importance of godparents than it previously did. Yet we lose something valuable if we let go of the idea of godparents. It is not so much during childhood that godparents matter; they come into their own later on. Nor are they exclusive to those who have been baptized as infants. Ask anybody, and they will probably be able to tell of one or two other people, fifteen to twenty years older than themselves, whose friendship has been good and strong.

For so the collective memory of how we learn to cope with life passes down from hand to hand. Collectively we edit our experience and try to pass on life as we think it should be, rather than all the pain of it that we suppress in our individual memories. At its crudest, this editing reveals itself in the saying that your schooldays are the happiest days of your life. We may like to look back and pretend that this was so. To do that says little for what we have made of our lives thereafter. For older people find it very hard to tell the young honestly how they felt as they fumbled their way through their teens. They have perhaps forgotten how they felt, and in their recollection smoothed away much of the hurt.

The conspiracy is not total. Schools have their counselling services, and as one seventeen-year-old put it, the suggestion is that "if you haven't considered suicide by the age of thirteen, you've got problems". Magazines for teenagers have their problem pages, encouraging their readers to pour out their miseries, and the agony aunts, such as Cathy and Clare of *Jackie*, take seriously complaints from growing girls whose mothers won't let them have their ears pierced.

All this may sound as if nowadays there is an openness about the difficulties that adolescents experience. Yet the adults who years ago came through their teens and are now on good terms with life easily underestimate how serious are these cries for help from the thickets of adolescence. "It is only a phase" they reckon. "We have all been through it, and you will soon come through."

Pop lyrics may know their audience better. "I was happy in the haze of a drunken hour, but heaven knows, I'm miserable now" sang the Smiths, as they worked their way up the charts. The message of many pop songs is "Don't be surprised to find that your life is wretched" and as they put their twenty pence pieces into the juke box in the corner of the pub, under-age kids sipping their illicit alcohol find their consolation.

Pop singers may cater for the market, but older people in any position of responsibility hardly dare warn the young that they should not be surprised if they feel lonely. Instead, families, school, neighbourhood, and all that activity laid on for youth, give the pretence that it is one big party, and the important thing is to take part. The advertisements that provide the teenage magazine with its profits have a far more powerful message than the problem page! "Belong! And if you want to be a success, wear this make-up, buy these records, choose these clothes. Do what the others are doing." For to commerce the teenage market is important, with pocket money and hard-earned pin money waiting to be spent.

Belong, through all your heartbreak and uncertainty, hang on in and it will all be all right. The immense orchestra playing its relentless signature tune "Belong" says to the bewildered young person, "We know. We are the sum of experience and we invite you to share it. Welcome, young person, to the dance floor of life. This is the tune; now learn to dance to it. You cannot sit out the dance, and surely you do not want to spend all your life as a wallflower. Listen to the rhythm, equip yourself with everything you need, and take your turn on the floor."

For it is so dark outside. That is the shadowy world of miseries and misfits, and who wants to be out there with them? That way madness lies. So the young person, boy or girl, follows the pied piper. The time of childhood has passed, and the cycle of life catches its newest victims. Nervously, or with a bit of brag, the young person tries out the steps. The music never stops and there is no interval on the programme for anyone to step outside and make friends with themselves.

Just at the age when they first need to be able to do it, young people are discouraged from exploring their own loneliness. Any twinges of it are to be laughed off, as "just a phase". For in the commerce of the world that they are entering, loneliness has no market value. The world is always suspicious of poets and artists, those who are prepared to go off on their own private expeditions. It wants everybody to join in, and take no notice of the shadow of loneliness that lurks in the gleam of the spotlight. Any move to explore that loneliness within is branded as anti-social.

Society has various hosts and hostesses whose business is to encourage the young person to take part. Traditionally religion has been one of the most powerful, with its ancient admission ceremonies to full membership. The Christian child is brought to confirmation, the Jewish boy goes to his bar-mitzvah, old enough now to read the scroll and form one of a community of ten that is the minimum needed for a synagogue. The bar-mitzvah proclaims his membership of that, just as confirmation emphasizes an individual commitment to belong. Conventionally used in the Church of England as the gateway to Holy Communion, confirmation says that now you should expect to spend the rest of your adult life as an active member of this body.

So good children set out to do. Before they have really had enough experience of life to find out what that commitment is likely to mean for them, they give their assent and are enrolled. Thus organized religion catches the young teenagers' natural desire to become full members of a body that until now has treated them as children. It may express that enrolment as making a personal commitment to Christ, and a reasonably intelligent young person can perfectly well see what that is meant to mean. It says that the world is much bigger than you are, and by making this commitment you will put yourself in trust to the God of the universe as he has shown himself to us in the person of Jesus. It says that, and wants at the same time to say that now you need never be afraid of feeling lonely. The person to whom you are committing your life has far more power and resource than you can imagine to make your little scrap of life whole and fulfilled.

There are indeed many Christians who can look back upon their confirmation in their early teens and see it as a step in what has for them remained a lifelong commitment. Their understanding of their faith may have changed and developed through the years, but the promises they made then remain valid for them.

For far more young people, confirmation in the early teens was their last act of childish conformity. That was what everybody expected, and they had no hesitation in obliging. A few years later, and they look back upon a moment of mistake. Now, as they approach adulthood, they have no wish to be saddled with all that religion. Church is boring. Later, perhaps, when they have children of their own, they may come back to it. For the moment, it has no hold upon them. Whatever sparkle of faith it was meant to fan, it apparently failed to catch.

Some Christian traditions put the moment of full membership later, around the age of eighteen rather than thirteen.

Then it is a rite of passage into adult life, rather than adolescence. So those who defer their commitment until that age are more likely to stay with it. Early teens are the time for the first small stabs at rebellion, and in so many ways not at all the right moment for being adopted into membership of the Church. Late teens are the time for staking one's own pitch in life, religious allegiance and all.

Late teens are also the moments when cults and other demanding causes go hunting for their recruits. On the streets and in the cafés the missionaries of Rev. Mr Moon and Hare Krishna go seeking for converts. By that age those who are likely to be seduced by them have experienced several years of pain as they pass through their teens, trying to find out how to belong. If they have failed, they wonder who they really are and how they can hitch on to a world that does not seem to make them at home. Behind their uncertainty lies the spectre of loneliness. Life cannot be meant to be as black as this; and yet it is. So that when somebody catches them on the raw with an invitation to total commitment and a complete sense of purpose, they are very vulnerable. Here at last is a group of friendly people who have found an aim in life and want to share it. At last everything can make sense.

Sharon was such a girl. Mum and Dad had rejected her, she was fat and unattractive. She felt on the edge of everything, when a chance encounter in the street brought her into the welcoming haven of a Moonie safehouse. Oh, it was miserable enough once she was past that first enfolding welcome. Not enough sleep, not enough food, meaningless, humiliating punishments; but she was convinced of a sense of her own awfulness, and somehow all this breaking of her spirit seemed part of a healing process. She had found a cause to commit herself to, others equally committed, and she must swallow all the infliction of misery and be grateful for it. For now she was on the first steps of a way of life that would be wholly fulfilling. Three years later, friends managed to rescue Sharon, to "deprogramme" her, and help her, at the age of twenty-one, to stumble back into the light and shade of the everyday world. "Now I can begin to be me again", she says. "I don't like it very much, but at least it is me."

Only a tiny handful of very young men and women fall into the arms of the cults. They tend to come from caring homes, and in rebelling against them, they are exposed to the appeal of organizations that seem to offer a better aim in life. The materialism of home all leads nowhere. Inside the haven of the cult, there is a fresh sense of purpose and achievement. Within weeks they are broken, within months restored to a new vision of life in which the old world out there is corrupt, but here all is point and purpose. The cliff of attainment is steep, with the high peaks of attainment way up in the clouds. But others are straining and scrambling their way up too, and those who have climbed higher beckon. After two or three years of that intoxication, youngsters take a great deal of rescuing.

Young people who fall victim to the cults have been unable during their teens to begin to come to terms with themselves. They have been frightened off, and fall headlong into a cruel nursery that is ready to exploit them for its own purposes. The sects make their appeal to a certain type of young person, those with a sense of high ideals that has so far found no fulfilment. Far more others, for whom life has always been rougher, find other causes to latch on to. They get themselves tattooed, they go into the world of punk and wear coxcombs, they are bikers. All these activities offer their members a chance to find mates and cock a snook at the stuffy world. So-called football hooligans are expressing their common protest at a world that has no room for them. Running amok together, causing damage and expressing their pent up violence is their way of saying "To hell with the whole system, I have my mates and together we will show you what we think of you all." That way, in the short run, they can squash all their sense of inadequacy and loneliness.

Or then there are causes. CND and Anti-Apartheid are the most obvious examples of simple causes that appeal particularly to young people. The old remark, "If you're not a Socialist at the age of eighteen, you have no heart ..." can express itself today in the words, "If you are not a member of CND in your teens ..." For all the complexities of the arguments for and against British unilateral nuclear disarmament, a young person can see very clearly the nonsense and the horror of a nuclear arms race, and here is an organization that shouts against it, and invites peaceful protest. So let us get the bus to Aldermaston, let us follow Mgr Bruce Kent on his long walk from Faslane to Burghclere, and then at least we shall have done something to show that we care. Whatever happens, we are in no danger of being lonely.

Then there are those young people who alarm their families and others with a care for them because they are solitary. The gang feels threatened by the one who does not belong. Their solitude may be a matter of temperament. The teenage boy in *Kes* who found himself through taming a kestrel is a good witness from fiction to the solitary who comes through. John throughout his teens never seemed to make friends. He came home, was always the one who would never join in what the rest of his family were doing, and seemed quite content with his own company. He had plenty of interests of his own, and spent hours working with his stereo and building up his music centre. Friends did not matter to him. Then came his late teens and he blossomed. He had found his interest, spent a year getting a technical qualification, and he was away. He would have laughed at anybody who suggested that he might be suffering from loneliness. He was quite content with his own company. Now, in his early twenties, he can go on and be himself, perfectly well satisfied with the circle of acquaintance that he makes through his electrical work.

For others the solitude is darker. Edged out of the gang, the group, they turn in upon themselves. They put up a front of not minding, and feed upon their isolation. Unable to bear other people's readiness to stretch out a hand of sympathy, they wade through waves of self-pity. Nobody cares, they reckon, and nobody understands.

At the extreme, teenagers try to commit suicide, and some succeed. Adrian was a gifted young man, well on his way to a commission at Sandhurst. He went out into the woods and shot himself. "I can't keep this up any longer" was the message of the note that he left. Everybody was horrified. Outwardly he was easy, pleasant, confident, nothing of the recluse. Inside, all the private turmoil led him to take his own life. For every Adrian, there are several young individuals who toy with the idea. "I am fifteen, and what is the meaning of life?" "Tomorow is my seventeenth birthday and I cannot bear another moment of this hypocrisy." There is nobody around the house, and it is so easy to turn on the gas. It is a long afternoon, and by the time anybody gets back it will be too late. But, no! They twiddle the tap, and there is daylight outside, and no.

These are dark moments. Nobody who has lived through them cares to remember them. In the accepted picture of life, such black prospects have no place. As we get older, and make our own compromises with the business of living, we dare not remember, let alone tell anybody, that somewhere in the wilderness of our adolescence, we thought of killing ourselves.

So society keeps up its conspiracy. Life is there for fulfilment. Belong, and make the most of yourself. Never admit that you had those anguished hours "… a stranger and afraid, In a world you never made." To admit that would spoil the party. All our business, each in our own different way, is to keep the show on the road. For anybody, especially when they are coming in as fully-fledged members of the circus, to want to drop out, is to cast doubt on the whole performance. We dare not allow that. It is all touch-and-go as it is.

We are therefore never taught how to be lonely. Discussion of loneliness hardly finds a place in even the most imaginative school curriculum. Health education and so on are all labelled social studies. If there are sessions with professionals from outside, and a consideration of deviant behaviour, it is couched in terms of how the alienated or the underprivileged behave. The thought that any one of us might feel lost and behave in such ways, is too dangerous.

3.

Grown Up and Alone

"I feel so lonely, I could scream." This is Ron, in his mid-twenties. "When I stand up, when I sit down, when I turn round, I cannot bear to be inside my skin. That's what I mean by being lonely." His loneliness is not just adolescent uncertainty about who you are. Ron is beyond that, he reckons. He knows only too well who he is, and he is not going to become anybody else. That he is lonely is the sum of what he knows. Indoors, out and about, wherever he is, his cloud of loneliness occupies his whole being. There is no room for anything else, no room for himself. Himself is his Siamese twin of loneliness, and Ron is on his own.

By their mid-twenties, at latest, young men and young women expect to have left home. Ronnie Corbett in "Sorry", somewhere past forty and still living with his parents, is a figure of fun. The days are long gone when unmarried daughters were expected to live at home, and grown up bachelor sons certainly reckon to go off and make their own way in the world. Households where a middle-aged couple still have any of their adult offspring living at home are rare indeed.

Far more familiar now is the pattern where the young move out, not too far away, perhaps, from their parents, and seeing them every so often. Despite laundrettes, there are still young men who take their dirty linen home for Mum to wash and iron. Yet a time is likely to come when even the most indulgent mother will complain about doing the laundry for her son. Most young people do not wait to be edged out. When they were first earning they were contributing something to the running of the home. Now they can keep that money towards the rent on at least a bedsit. There they can come and go as they please, there they can make the place their own, there they can be themselves.

The process of moving away from home used to have much more to do with finding a marriage partner. In all classes of society custom, or economic necessity, kept unmarried young adults under the family roof. Couples who met and became engaged would expect to wait two or three years to save up for a place of their own. Even now, young couples have a deep reluctance to begin life together under her Mum's roof. As soon as possible, a young person expects to leave home, and social pressures urge the move. Any young people still living with their parents once their studying days are done now seem something of a freak. They are to be pitied, if not despised. Parents have come to feel that their young are not grown up until they have left home.

This pattern is not confined to native English people. Ask anyone working in housing, and they will say that even immigrants of south Asian background now begin to behave in the same way. The conventional picture of four generations crowded under one roof is less and less accurate. Their young people, like others, want to move out as soon as they can. Without necessarily waiting to set up home with a long-term partner of their own choosing, they want their own place. They are ready to make their own mark on the world.

Convention still assumes that their next business is to marry and live happily ever after. A royal wedding is a glittering reminder of how it is all meant to be. Even the Japanese bride who, having watched such a wedding on television in Tokyo, and came to London to marry the man her parents had chosen, wanted one of those. The ritual by which a man and a woman pledge themselves to one another, amidst all those trappings, has a very deep appeal. For all but a few, who early dedicate themselves to a celibate life, such as monks or missionaries or artists, the peal of wedding bells touches an echoing chord.

Then there are homosexual partnerships. The perfect ones last as well as any conventional marriage. Tom and Duncan had been together as long as anybody in the street could remember. They were both retired now, and their abiding support for one another was a model which even the most critical neighbours could not help admiring.

It does not always happen like that, it does not always happen at the appropriate moment, and it does not always last. So there are very many people, of all sorts of social backgrounds, who find themselves going through their twenties, away from their families and on their own. It may be for the sake of their career or simply to get away. So there they are on their own. Till not so long ago they might have expected to find digs with a landlady. Landladies became substitute mothers, dishing up stew and greens, and complaining about too much noise. Landladies were a stock subject for music-hall jokes, but when did anybody last hear one? As a breed, they are fast disappearing.

Instead the houses where boarders used to sit round the kitchen table, before removing themselves to their rooms with their slot-machine gasfires, have become "multiple occupancies". Each room has its own lock, and a curtained-off Baby Belling next to the all-purpose basin. From out of them mutual strangers emerge to go to the bathroom. Stew and greens made a household, which instant packet meals do not.

So commerce adapts itself to the requirements of the market. The majority of private landlords letting off single rooms no doubt provide a reasonable service, but the name of Rachman has entered into the language. With inadequate public regulation to ensure a decent standard of service in small dwelling units, and the Fair Rent Act hedged by daunting bureaucracy, young adults who are for the first time trying to live on their own are at the mercy of the market. They are fair game, too, for loneliness.

Many of them, for the sake of mutual protection if nothing more, will share a flat with two or three others. Whether all its members are of the same sex, or mixed, such households are common enough. Any newsagent's window carries its small advertisement for "Third girl wanted" as individuals come and go. Unless those who remain are unusually choosy, it is never too difficult to find someone else to make up the number, and so such billets may last long after their original members have all left. They are informal youth hostels, and so long as anyone is prepared to muck in and pay their way, they can belong for a while. Nobody has to be particularly intimate, or say more than they want to about themselves.

Such households make somewhere to live. They are hardly home. The furniture and fittings are somebody else's. A cushion or two, posters stuck on the wall, make brave efforts to identify the place with its occupiers. For the time being it will do. For some it may do quite well. In particular those whose upbringing has been in institutional care may jump for joy at this first chance to feather their own nests. For people away for the first time from home comforts, it claims to be no more than a temporary pad.

Not many local councils expect to provide accommodation for people living on their own. As a category, they keep falling to the bottom of the housing list. In some places enterprising housing associations have stepped in to turn family dwellings into homes, where half a dozen single people can live at moderate rent and enjoy some sort of common-room life. There is always the telly to be shared. These associations may have a policy of letting their accommodation to those under the age of, say, thirty, recognizing that it is hard to make ages mix, and that young adults are likely to do better if they are with a group of contemporaries. Older single people are more set in their ways, and may well infect those younger than themselves with their own lonely jaundice.

For it is not so much a question of comfort. It is a question of purpose. The most uncomfortable army barrackroom, the roughest cabin on a works site, can make perfectly happy homes from home because there is a reason for being there. The bedsit, by contrast, is a road-side campsite, and who knows where the road is supposed to lead? It can look as if it is leading nowhere, and a pitch on the road to nowhere has no comfort to offer.

So there all the conditions are right for loneliness to breed. Why am I here? Where am I going? Who are all these other people? What have they to do with me? People on their own, away from all that has previously given them security, find these questions staring back at them from the chipped mirror, and it is all so pointless.

A generation ago there was a whole literature of the absurd, that explored this question of pointlessness. Much of it was in French: not only Sartre, but the novels of Albert Camus. In *The Stranger* and *The Plague* he created anti-heroes; instead of inviting the reader to warm to his central characters, he made them unappealing, yet compelling, in their tortuous anguish. Then Samuel Beckett, in his plays, took the exploration further. *End Game* and *Waiting for Godot* are two of the best-known. With their surrealist situations, they drill with pity and humour into desperate human efforts to make sense where there is none. The only props are half-remembered rules for a game whose purpose has long been forgotten, if indeed it ever had one.

Beckett's plays still draw full houses when they are revived, and evidently touch tender nerves. This is theatre doing what all sorts of gurus investigate when they invite their followers to learn a particular technique of meditation. Without theatre, and without a guru, the loneliest person can begin on the journey of self-discovery.

Anyone can begin by taking stock of their surroundings. Here I am. This is me. There is nobody else around. If there are others, they are shadowy figures. This is me, here, all on my own.

Even the most miserable me is not suspended in space. There is a body, arms and legs. There is breathing, and air to breathe, and blood pounding purposefully round. There is space, space for movement. I can stretch, move my limbs, walk, go from here to there. I can do this even if I am Ron, carting my burden of loneliness. Yes, even when I reach there, I am still here, for I am always here, and I can never be anywhere else. Here it is always now, and it can never be then. It *was* then, but that is no longer now. Now is the moment in which I am, and where I always have been and where I shall be for the rest of my life.

For I am who I was, am I not? I am who I shall be. Simply to stretch the lines of this "I" into the remembered past and into the unknown future is to spread and be somewhat more than the merciless mirror at this instant reflects.

But all this is "I" in a vacuum, and whatever I am, I am not just I in a vacuum. There is otherness all around, otherness that goes on and out, that was here long before I was, and will be around for ever so long after I am not. This otherness appears indifferent to me, but I relate to it and depend upon it. Not only is there the air that I breathe, and the pulse of life which keeps my blood coursing, and the space in which I move and the light by which I see. Beyond that there is more. For I am neither in a vacuum, nor a castaway in space, but beneath my feet there is ground. On that I put all my weight. If I lie down, and relax totally, the ground holds me. The forces of nature, the law of gravity, call them what I may, they keep me in place. I am not weightless, not disembodied. Though I let myself go totally, still they keep me in place. Still all this frame sustains me, as it sustains everything, as it sustains other people.

So I lie there and let my breath go, and keep my lungs empty as long as I can. In a moment or two my brain will start pounding and I shall have to take another breath. Meanwhile I am aware of my emptiness, of my dependence. I let go of everything, I let go of my loneliness. It may not go away, but the weight of it goes. For in that emptiness, that solitude, that silence in which the hum of the world recedes, loneliness becomes velvet-pawed.

Lying flat, relaxed and dependent, letting the brain slow right down until it is only just ticking over, I begin to let go of "I". As that I subsides, isolation becomes domesticated. No longer is there this usual conscious person, chained to a burden of loneliness. Instead there is just a living and dependent being, in its natural state of isolation. It is quite different from staring into the mirror, watching breath come and go on the glass. In the mirror lie self-pity, self-doubt, and, hovering some way behind them, madness. They are the spectres who make it feel impossible for Ron to live within his own skin. By relaxing completely, he has a chance to accept himself at home in the otherness of the world.

One great business of religion is to give this process of relaxation its scaffolding. For the moment of relaxation and acceptance becomes the moment of thanks. Life is a gift, to be accepted with gladness. Call the giver by whatever name you like, and through that name express your thanks – thanks for the air, the space, for yourself and your mind and body in it. Soon the thanks spread out into the remembered world; for the rhythm of the seasons and their fruit that provides food and drink, warmth and shelter; thanks for those who brought you up. To be able to say "thank you" is the first defence against loneliness, and against its cousin, despair.

Thanks is not just for all the external things. Everything good is gift – brains, ability, imagination, just as much as the air we breathe or the blood that runs in our veins. Look in the mirror, and it is easy to think of all these as possessions – my brains, my wit, my talents, all capable of being listed in an inventory of things that I own. Down on the floor, that catalogue crumbles. There is no I who can proudly claim ownership; these natural abilities are all given to us, as much as the surroundings in which they can be exercised; and again the appropriate thing is to give thanks for them.

But then what about effort, all the energy that goes into making the most of these gifts? Isn't that at least something that I can really claim as my own, something on which I can congratulate myself? It seems very unfair not to be able to label that as all my own work, with no thanks to anybody else.

Des is a paraplegic. He was an athletic young man, charming and great fun, until at the age of eighteen he had a severe motor cycle injury that left him brain-damaged and with severe physical handicaps. Before that injury, with a bright future in the Royal Navy ahead of him, he might well have thought that he owed his achievements and his prospects to his own efforts. Then, smash! Some years later, there he is, walking with the aid of a stick, with no realistic prospect of much further recovery, or of ever being able to go out into the world and make a living. His great delight is his skill on the pool table, and he spends hours practising. Out of the mess of his accident he has retrieved this one precious skill. Surely he can claim that as his own. Then a few years ago he would have naturally claimed the rest as his own, and he has forfeited them. Somehow even the effort that we expend to make the most of ourselves cannot be counted as our own property. That, too, is a matter for thanksgiving.

Yet to lie on the floor, aware of little more than a sense of dependence and isolation, and of thanksgiving, does bring to the surface the bubbles of dissatisfaction. Our muscles are relaxed, from the toes upwards, and from the finger-tips, till finally we are relaxing our brains almost to the point of forgetting ourselves. All we are aware of by now is a being that is nobody else, breathing, and sustained, and here.

There is stillness, and within all the void that invites others, there is this being who is nobody else but me. The relaxation may have lasted a few minutes, a quarter of an hour – it does not too much matter how long. Then there rises to the brim this awareness of my own not quite fitting, not being quite at ease, not being exactly as I should be. I cannot quite believe in myself as I am, for the mess of it all is somehow all of my own making.

To say that if only we could magic away our mess we would lose our loneliness is far too pat. Yet there is a parallel. We are not meant to make a muck of things, but we do. We are not meant to be lonely, but we are. Everything in us cries out to be accepted, not rejected; to be loved, not to be lonely. We cannot snap out of loneliness when we have no expectation of love.

Richard became very lonely around the age of thirty. He was living alone, half way round the world from his family in Australia, and suddenly it seemed as if all his friends had deserted him. If he did ring up some old pal and make a date, he could hardly bring himself to keep the appointment, for fear of being rejected once more. He could hardly bear to go to work, he could not bring himself to go shopping. He spent evening after evening sitting in his room. He did not want to watch television. He could not abide the chatter of the radio. He could barely read two pages of a book. Even dealing with the ordinary affairs of living was too much for him. It was all a mockery.

In desperation he rang the Samaritans. The friendly voice at the other end of the line seemed to be the first human being with whom he had made any real contact for months and months. The next night he rang again, and out of the hard crust of his loneliness began to speak more easily. He had been in the acting world, and was enough of a professional to observe the physical changes in his behaviour. His throat muscles were starting to relax. His voice was beginning to sound more like he had always thought it did. He was no longer clutching the phone, but learning to treat it as a convenient tool rather than a sinister weapon. He even began to wander about the room with it, in the way that he had been used to doing. Suddenly he heard himself laugh, and for him that laughter was an explosion. He had forgotten laughter. In the lonely world good laughter has no citizenship.

From that moment of laughter onwards, things moved fast. It was not long before Richard was accepted as a potential Samaritan himself, and soon to his astonishment he found himself on the rota and in regular demand. At first he almost wished that they would let him be on call every evening, but they had more sense than that. So a couple of nights a week at first, and later on three, he had the unexpected pleasure of sitting in waiting for phone calls that were certain to come. Previously the ring of his telephone had been something that he dreaded but needed. A ring in those days had meant that at least somebody else out there was interested in him enough to dial his number. It also meant that he had to respond in a way that would conceal his loneliness, for otherwise they would never ring again. On the whole it was easier when nobody rang. Sometimes he used to take his phone off the hook to make sure that they could not.

Now all that changed. The phone was certain to ring, but the caller would be somebody in distress needing his attention and care. Instead of having to conceal his own loneliness, and affect a bright artificial interest, Richard was now able to be himself. His business was largely to listen, but when the caller came to a pause, to say just enough to encourage further confidences. His greatest satisfaction was when he managed to make the other person laugh.

To somebody who is obstinately lonely, Richard's story may sound too good to be true. It almost belongs to the circle of brisk advice – get out and embrace life. The difference is that he had not done that. Instead he had wallowed in the slough of despond, and from that pit made his cry for help. In Jesus's story of the prodigal son the young man first "wasted his substance in riotous living". After that he had no choice but to attach himself to a farmer to look after his pigs, and he became so hungry that "he fain would eat the husks that the swine did eat". One thing that we hardly notice in the story is the horror that a Jewish audience would feel to think of a wastrel working with pigs. So he really had reached bottom when at last "he came to himself".

Richard "came to himself". For lonely people the natural complaint is that they are cut off from everybody else, and have only themselves for company. They might sneer at the phrase "came to himself". For them, it seems, there is nowhere else to come, and they are there already, there all the time. Locked inside their own skins, that ache every time they move, where else are they but deep inside themselves? The story of the prodigal son suggests something more. He was lonely enough, and on his beam ends, as he sat minding his guzzling pigs, full of remorse, full of self-pity. But if we take the story as St Luke records it, there was another stage. Through all that misery and despair, he came to himself.

Loneliness keeps its iron grip upon those who are afraid to come to themselves. They may, like the young man in the parable, be looking back to times not so long ago when it was all fun. There were the parties, drinks all round, and the company, and no time to wonder about things. Then there was a famine in the land – and how many people can blame circumstances for their plight! It is not my fault that I'm lonely. If I hadn't lost my job, if there weren't all this unemployment, if that wretched man hadn't walked off with my girl, I would not be in this mess. It's not my fault.

All sorts of circumstances can land somebody in their mid-twenties on the lonely scrap heap. Men who have done their nine years in the forces, and decide to try their fortunes back in civvy street, can find themselves wandering round on their own in a world that is unfamiliar and hostile. All the natural mateyness of barrackroom life has gone. Or consider Caroline, who was musical. Once qualified, she did what so many music students do, and got a job teaching. She always saw it as a temporary step, since her ambition was to play in an orchestra, so she never became an enthusiastic member of the school staff. Instead, she taught her pupils, and longed for the day when she could leave. At last a chance came, and she got a temporary job in an orchestra. From there, she thought, she could soon find a permanent post. It was harder than she thought, and she found herself back in her bedsit with only her violin for company. Every Saturday she scanned the *Daily Telegraph* for orchestral vacancies, and applied for every post that she could. Occasionally she was invited for an audition, but months and months went by and she never got offered a place. Each rejection made her more and more miserable. She could hardly bear to practise, and began to lose confidence in herself as a musician. She even looked back with nostalgia upon her time as a teacher. At least there had been other staff around, and even though she had made no effort to be at home amongst them, it had been somewhere to belong. To go back to teaching now would be the end of her ambition. To go home to her family in the North would be a total admission of defeat. Almost the biggest event in her lonely life was the fortnightly visit to the unemployment benefit office. Standing in the dole queue, all she could see were other individuals each shut inside their own distress.

Caroline's story may not ring too many bells. At least she always had her violin. She had a skill, and one that she could exercise even when she was on her own. So many lonely people come to wonder whether they are good at anything, or good for anything. They may be earning their livings, they may have a trade or some other qualification, but what use are those when you are back on your own in the evenings, behind closed doors? They are only a means to earning a living, and what is the use of means without an end in view?

"The chief end of man", says the seventeenth-century Westminster Confession, "is to praise God and enjoy him for ever." There have been plenty of jokes about sitting down on man's chief end, but for so many people these booming words are no joke. They conjure up pictures of twanging a harp for eternity, and that seems sick fantasy. How can they possibly be translated into language that makes sense to anybody who has been frightened off God and sees praise as meaningless flattery?

It is not easy to translate these words into down-to-earth English, for down-to-earth ignores the world beyond that they take for granted. What they are saying is that each one of us is made for a purpose, and our business is to fulfil it. There is no convenient docket to tell us what that purpose is. Anyone whose life is outwardly in a mess may laugh at the idea that there can possibly be any purpose in it.

But lonely young adults may have a better chance than many other people to find out what they are for and what is the purpose of their lives. By plunging into the depths of their own loneliness, they may come to themselves. Caroline's story has its point. It was not until many years afterwards that she could look back on her months of despair and recognize what was really wrong. Now that she can do so, she can speak of it in terms of refusing to come to herself, and instead trying to live with this mocking image of what she ought to be. That is what trapped her in her loneliness. She was hanging on at all costs to her picture of herself as a successful musician, ready to sacrifice everything for the sake of her ambition. What she came so perilously near to sacrificing was herself and her own sanity. It was only by exorcizing that devil of ambition that she began to find her own true worth, and make a fresh start. "These days," she says, "I am kinder to myself, and perhaps just a little bit more honest."

4.

And In the Prime of Life

The last group of people that we would naturally expect to be lonely are those aged between, say, thirty and forty-five. By that age, men and women, they have set their stamp on life and are on the way to making the most of themselves. Anyone in those years who suffers from loneliness, it is tempting at first to feel, must be sick, or a misfit. These are busy years, years of making good in a career, of bringing up a family, of improving a home, of being busy with the feeling of a long way still to go. For normal men and women, there is simply no time to be lonely.

It is to people at this stage of life that so much general advertising appeals. There they are, father and mother, with two children and a dog, finding their lives transformed by purchasing this house, that car, those appliances, and doing their washing with the new improved powder. Advertising insists that the sun is always shining, that the grass is even greener in the next field, and that happiness and sociability is the birthright of us all, so long as we use our money in the desired way.

Advertising abhors loneliness as nature abhors a vacuum. Of course lonely people have to eat and clothe themselves, and need somewhere to live, so they must spend money. But the world to which general advertising makes its appeal is one in which people spend money with an eye to others. The family household is therefore its largest and most easily identifiable market. Yet even the advertising that appears to appeal to one individual – and that includes a wide variety of specialist advertising – is still looking over the potential customer's shoulder to see who else might be interested. The person who is being urged to buy a new camera is going to take photographs of other people, and show them off when they have been developed and printed. The prospective purchaser of a home computer is going to demonstrate the new acquisition. Advertising depends upon us all spending money in ways that other people will notice. Nobody is going to notice how the lonely person spends money.

Yet loneliness also knows its way into the same market. Those who are most obviously lonely in these years of young maturity are those whose marriages have collapsed. There are many of them about. The gaudy picture that we have of one partner rushing off with somebody else, leaving the other one stranded, is now less typical than the pair who simply part. After somewhere between ten and twenty years of marriage, they can no longer stand the strain of one another. A woman who has borne and raised her children to the point where they are more or less able to stand the strain of a split home yearns to make something else of her life, and the thought of spending the rest of it as an appendage to her husband and his career may fill her with growing horror.

It is not difficult, as it once was, for her to make a fresh start on her own. If she has some qualification or work experience already, it is not going to be impossible for her to earn her own living. Whether lawyers are involved or not, the man and wife will divide their possessions, and if they have a house to sell, she will be able to take her share of the proceeds and so start again.

Couples who split in this way shut the matrimonial door behind them and risk walking straight into the arms of loneliness. It may not be there immediately. The signs of relief at being free and the satisfactions of creating a new home of one's own, however much more modest it may be than the joint one, can postpone the rendezvous. The comfort of friends who suspected that it would never last but did not like to say so provides a heady tonic. Loneliness is in no hurry. It is prepared to wait until the children have set up on their own and said goodbye to these relics of homes. It is ready to take its chance at empty weekends, when the decorating has been done and friends have other things to do. It is quite ready to be a night-time visitor, when there is nobody else about. It may even be there in the morning, peering out of the mirror above the washbasin.

Impatiently the newly separated man or woman orders the monster down. This, they remind themselves, is the new life that I have chosen, or at any rate accepted with as good grace as I can muster. It may be very silent, but at least I can please myself. There is no longer that awful tension of those bad years, when it grew harder and harder to know how to communicate with one another. We are now, each of us, single people, one of us here, one of us there. This is what we have agreed to do, because we had the honesty to admit that we could no longer go on together. It is sad that we can no longer say "we", immeasurably sad; but "we" cannot, and now it is a matter of learning how to say "I" once more. And if "I" never considered myself lonely in the past, all those years ago, before we set about trying to become "we" why should I give way to loneliness now?

With such brave thoughts, those who have separated address themselves. Yet bravery runs the risk of suppressing and delaying the onset of loneliness, and in the end it may pounce far more fearsomely. For separation is a bereavement, and just as those who lose a partner by death need to be able to grieve, so do those who have lost one by separation.

It is a harder grief to bear. Those whose partners have died are gradually able to piece together a bitter-sweet mosaic of memory. Those who have parted from their partners, with half their lives still to live, cannot so easily find this consolation. They may recall happy times not so very many years ago, but all the time they have to ask themselves how that led to this. They may find continuing comfort from their children, who with amazing grace ride this shattering of all their security. The newspaper stories of tugs of love usually refer to young children whom anguished and embittered parents use as barter. Any couple that parts a little later in life is more likely to have a somewhat older family – and questions of custody and access are no longer so dominant. Even so, it is foolish for separated parents to treat their children as receptacles for their private loneliness. The children have enough suffering of their own, and whoever is to blame for the collapse of the marriage, it is not them.

Blame and self-reproach are the ingredients that make separation a harder grief than natural bereavement. Natural bereavement produces its share of those feelings. Particularly if a death is unexpected, those who are left may sooner or later find themselves feeling guilty. "If only I hadn't behaved like that ..." and "I should have done so-and-so." That is painful guilt, because it is absolutely too late to amend. In separation the blame and self-reproach spread wider. The whole enterprise of marriage has sunk, and at so many points on its past voyage lie recollected reefs and sandbanks. Oh, to have avoided them then, to have taken another course at that point, and day by day by day to have steered in a way that would have kept the sails full for our lifetime together! Oh, and now it is irretrievable!

In another way too separation opens its windows to the blasts of loneliness. There is no socially accepted ritual of sympathy. With a death, there is a funeral, and all the halting expressions of compassion. Separation has no claims upon anything like that. Neighbours feel that they have been duped. Shared friends retire to decide with which, if either, of the ex-partners their loyalties now lie. Colleagues and workmates of either do not know what to say. Even if they could find words to express their warmth of feeling, the injured party might well be too sore to listen. At this stage neither of the couple can bear the intrusion of strangers into the suicide of their union. The last thing that they want to hear is some outsider's criticisms of the other. For the moment they are each locked into private worlds apart. It is almost as if they have each announced an engagement to loneliness.

If amongst those between the ages of thirty-five and fifty separating couples are the most obvious candidates for loneliness, they are by no means the only ones. Single women, particularly those who have till now dedicated themselves to their careers, are increasingly at risk as the years mount towards the point where they know that they can never have children of their own.

Linda was always determined to make a career for herself in publishing. She achieved a good degree, and quite a portfolio of undergraduate writing, so that a leading firm was prepared to give her a first post. She took to her work, and within a few years had established her reputation as a publisher's editor. To start with, she had shared a flat with two other women, but when she could afford it she bought a place of her own. Her work involved dealing with authors and their agents, and the usual round of publishing parties. In her twenties it never occurred to her to think that she was unhappy or unfulfilled. Pouring all her intellectual sensitivity into judging written words, socially she covered herself with bright charm, and everybody who knew her thought what an attractive young woman she was.

But her career was her life, and she took more and more pains to avoid any glimmer of emotional entanglement. She even gave up going home very often to her family, miles away in the country. Amongst her circle of acquaintance, her bright charm hardened. By the time she reached the age of thirty, they were beginning to think of her as hard. They were beginning not to think of her as a woman. The two with whom she had shared a flat had both got married and started families. At first they used to be glad to invite Linda to stay with them, but she refused pressing requests to become a godmother, showed no interest in the babies, and so let the friendships run to seed.

She had boasted that she never had a day's illness, but one winter when she was thirty-six she had a bad bout of flu. Suddenly there was nobody she could ring to bring her comfort. Suddenly it hit her how lonely she was. Mooching about her flat in the tedium of convalescence, she tried to absorb herself in the latest manuscript. Its words stared dully from the page. She reminded herself that depression was a well-known after-effect of flu, and decided to treat herself to a holiday. Sitting for a fortnight on her own on a Greek island she came face to face with her own loneliness.

Like the violinist Caroline, Linda had made her career her god. Unlike Caroline, she had been successful from the beginning. There was no question of admitting that she was not good enough, and crawling back down to a lower rung. She was successful, and now there was nothing else for it. In the process she had cut herself off from other people. She relied on no one else, and there was no one else that she cared about. She was lonely.

Then her widowed mother fell ill. At first she was in no hurry to summon her daughter, but Linda went to visit her, and after a few days' trial, settled in as nurse. Linda was fortunate. Though she could never fully admit to her mother her own sense of failure and her loneliness, the daily business of nursing had a healing effect. She had felt obliged to give her firm notice, and when eventually she did go back to work, she was glad to find a place in a different firm. Pacing herself there much more slowly, she developed a reputation as a sympathetic aunt. She kept well hidden her own searing brush with loneliness, but appreciated that that was what enabled her to listen to others.

For when loneliness breaks through the crust of those who thought that they had made good terms with life, it shatters all their illusions. They had seen themselves in charge, monitoring their relationships with other people, secure within the fortress of their own privacy. When the fortress releases its ghosts, their isolation becomes appalling. Privacy is no longer a faithful servant, but a Frankenstein.

Sir Peter Parker, sometime chairman of British Rail, gave a short talk in a Radio 4 series, "Last Words". In it he said that the most important final message he would want to leave his family was to remember their interdependence. He made the point that nowadays the young are encouraged to become independent. While that may be fine, he argued that the risk is that we forget how much we all depend upon one another. He was not only talking about family relationships, but the relationships within an organization, any place of work. There the "chieftains", as he put it, are in special danger of assuming that so much hangs on them, and indeed they may wake at three a.m. knowing that it is for them alone to make some important decision. Yet just as British Rail needs the dedication of the lonely railwayman who goes out in the snow to make sure that the line is clear, so in all our dealings we cannot pretend that we can manage without one another. E.M. Forster made the same point more succinctly: "Only connect."

Certainly we do each need to be private. When it was published in 1959, David Riesman's book *The Lonely Crowd* provided a generation with a new watchword. In Eisenhower's America, conformism ruled, and everybody was gulled into a feeling of inadequacy if they did not somehow manage to behave like everybody else. The Harvard sociologist's plea was for individual space in which people could have a chance to become themselves. Another book, Elie Canetti's *Crowds*, develops the theme. Written from Toronto, *Crowds* is an anthropologist's study of the ways that human beings behave en masse. In particular he observes how people behave on the edges of crowds, to detach themselves from the electricity that runs through them, and how in accidental crowds our instinct is to put an invisible hedge round ourselves. So, for instance, in an Underground train, without thinking about it we have developed an instinct for self-protection. Other bodies may jostle against our own, but we hold ourselves from them as much as we can. Equally, we restrain ourselves as far as possible from making embarrassing contact with them. Any unintended contact, and there is quick withdrawal; and especially we seek to avoid eye contact. Generally speaking, in that brief encounter, it is more than we can bear to exchange any sort of glance. Our privacy matters.

At first privacy and loneliness seem in direct relation. We have this instinct to be private, and it appears that if we indulge it too much, we walk into the trap of loneliness. Privacy, it seems, is of our own making, and we have the power to decide in any dealings precisely how little or how much of ourselves we mean to give away. Loneliness is clearly involuntary; nobody wants to be lonely.

Mature people certainly know the difference. One of the engaging things about young children is their openness. They are naturally ready to take any stranger into their confidence, and one of the hard lessons of social training is to teach them caution and reserve: "Never take sweets from a stranger." Mentally handicapped people preserve this childish openness. However battering their experience of living may be, their way is to go on greeting the world with a wide-eyed smile. The rest of us have learned the hard way. There are those who have gone to the other extreme, and "keep themselves to themselves". The rest of us regard them as tight and unfriendly, and yet everybody's diplomatic engagement with other people hangs upon adjusting the springs of privacy to match each fresh encounter.

In *Crowds* Canetti argues that most human beings are far

less in control of those springs than they care to imagine. We are all of us looking for the best appropriate level of encounter with those whom we meet. Experience of previous meetings gives us some guide to the measure of response that we can expect in any new one. Even the most coldly calculating mortal, wary of giving anything away, can hardly be in complete control of every meeting. The natural desire to get as much out of the meeting as possible, and to give as much to it, is checked by the fear of uneven response. We are as afraid of the response that is too gushing as we are of the cool one. So, with a set of behaviour tools hardened by use, at every encounter we are ready to fence until we have found the mutually satisfactory level for developing the meeting.

Our sense of privacy, then, owes more to instinct than we might care to imagine. It is as instinctive as the sense that warns us against putting our fingers too near the fire. Both are instincts, developed by experience, against getting hurt. It is when the instinct for privacy becomes self-conscious that it can get in the way of our relationships with other people. Anyone who feels that their privacy is threatened may start treating other people's advances as impertinence. They react as if a stranger is demanding of them more than they are prepared to give, and so they start putting up their defences and retreating into themselves. They do not want to know, and they do not want to be known. Eventually they may reach a point where they are unable to know, and unable to be known. That is the state of loneliness which mature people reach when wilfully they have cut themselves off from the give and take of everyday relationships. They have got into the state willingly enough, but find to their dismay that they cannot so easily will themselves out of it.

Reluctant as we are to admit to our own loneliness, we can learn something by taking the trouble to look at other people. We easily learn, for instance, to spot the difference between the chatterbox and the secretive person. Neither is a measure of how lonely they may feel. The chatterbox may well be ready to gossip to anybody whose attention can be attracted, so as to cover up the emptiness inside. People who chat away to nobody but themselves, as they stand at the bus stop or shuffle along the street, are familiar figures of pity. Talking to yourself is the first sign of madness, they used to say. It is certainly a very clear mark of loneliness.

The secretive person at least comes across as somebody with plenty of self-control. They may have long since come to terms with their own loneliness, and feel at ease with themselves. They have worked out what for them is a perfectly satisfactory truce with the world in which they find themselves living. They find little need to communicate, and their reserve has become second nature.

It is then a mistake to confuse privacy with loneliness. We all need to be private, but nobody needs to feel lonely. We need to feel private in order to sustain ourselves as sane persons. In the Latin from which it derives *persona* means a mask, such as actors wore, and as persons we do go masked. In our public roles, especially, we keep our masks on, and others do not expect us to take them off. The general practitioner, the bank manager, the school teacher, all owe their standing to a measure of masking, and that is what their clientele expects, and respects. To a greater or lesser degree, every one of us is required to go veiled, and it would be unbearable for others, as it would be for ourselves, if we refused to play the part.

We behave as persons towards other people, only ready to start taking off our veils in front of those with whom we are intimate. To the mirror we may pretend that we are unveiled, but even to ourselves we cannot bear to be stripped quite naked. "O, wad some Power the giftie gie us, To see oursels as ithers see us," said Robert Burns. It might be good for us all, but their views are distorted, too. Many of us would find it even more painful to see ourselves as we really are. For to strip away all the masks is to reveal our essential loneliness.

Yet how can we talk of our essential loneliness if at the same time we want to say that nobody need feel lonely? It is to do with the difference between states and feelings. To make a comparison, my state may be unhealthy: the tests that doctors could make would give telltale clues to do with weight, blood pressure and the rest. Yet I may not feel unhealthy. I may be so used to my physical condition that I give no thought to it. I expect to get out of breath after walking up a couple of flights of stairs; I take good care never to run for a bus; and by living within the limits of my unfitness, from day to day I have no sensation of being less healthy than I might be. Similarly, we can talk of our essential loneliness as the human condition. There is an underlying sense in which every one of us is lonely. Our relationships with others are far from perfect, and each one of us goes through life on our own, none of us a perfect fit for the world we inhabit. Yet many people make shift to manage without rubbing up very consciously against their essential loneliness. They are like the run of the human race, being medically less than fit, yet avoid confronting themselves with their unfitness.

To be told that everybody else is essentially lonely may be little consolation for those who feel their loneliness like an incurable toothache. It is all very well, they may think, to be told that actually everybody else is in the same state. Just look at them! They seem to be getting along perfectly happily, and how easily they mix with other people. They clearly do not feel lonely, and it is of no use saying that they really are. Those people who know that they are lonely know that their loneliness marks them out from the majority of the people around them, who, by every observable act, cannot possibly be feeling the same way. They look happy, they always have plenty to do, and plenty of other people glad to be in their company. For the lonely person it makes no sense to be told that actually everybody else is lonely too. It is as bad as telling people blind from birth that sight is really an illusion.

Yet for mature people facing their own loneliness it may be of some help to consider that their plight is not abnormal. For the great deceit of loneliness is to make the sufferer believe that nobody else can be experiencing just such pain. To suffer from a cold, or some other mild physical complaint, is not too painful, because we all know that other people have colds too. They survive them, and no doubt so shall we. To suffer from something more serious and long-lasting hurts that much more, but again there are other people around with a similar complaint and it is possible to compare notes. To suffer from loneliness is to doubt that anybody else can possibly have the same experience, and that is the root of its pain.

George was somebody who worked his way through to that discovery. For years he had enjoyed a stable homosexual relationship, until the day came when his partner inexplicably decided to go. George, well into his forties, did all the sensible things. He bought himself a little house, and took great pains to make it attractive. He made friends with the young couple across the street. He found a woman to come in twice a week and clean his house. He made sure that he had various regular evening engagements. All that he did, but still his loneliness bore in on him. Then he began trying to belong to a succession of quasi-religious organizations, and amused his young neighbours with his tales of them. They simply seemed to extract his money, or occupy him with humbling chores. For a few weeks the new one would offer the key to life which he thought he had previously not found, but soon too its disciplines and doctrines palled. And George became obsessed with his own loneliness. He began haunting the appropriate bars, but could never find anyone with whom he could begin to form even the beginnings of a satisfactory friendship. His laugh grew hollow, and his tales repetitive, and he seemed to be sunk in his loneliness.

For him relief came when he met another man, about his own age, who admitted to being lonely too. The admission did not come easily on either side, as the two of them jockeyed for position. But step by step they did begin to be able to talk of the experience of loneliness, and from there to build a lasting good friendship. George insists that it was talking of his loneliness to somebody in the same condition that helped him to face his own. Till then he had not dared to talk to anyone about it, or if he did, he made very light of it. When his young neighbours tentatively enquired whether he felt lonely, he would only say, "Oh, you get used to it" and they were left feeling that they had intruded on something that he preferred to conceal from them.

Only after he had established his new friendship was George ready to talk at all to anyone else of what he had gone through. The essence of it was simply not being able to believe that anybody else could be having the same experience. On the surface, he was sensible enough to realize that there must be thousands of other people around concealing a similar loneliness. But that only reinforced his own. For he was ashamed of it, as an awful secret to be kept well hidden from the world. So he nursed his shame, and took artificial pride in not letting anyone else know of it. Thus suppressed, his loneliness festered and would not let go of him until he had found somebody else with whom he could share it to the point where it disappeared.

5.

This Way Madness Lies

One of the undoubted advances of the last hundred years lies in the field of mental illness. Till the late nineteenth century those who called themselves pyschologists were speculative theoreticians. What they had to say about the study of the human mind did not bear very heavily on the work of the medical profession. So the classic way that Victorian society dealt with the moonstruck – lunatics – was to lock them away in asylums. For all societies mental derangement had always been frightening, and since the nineteenth century had witnessed the growth and spread of the belief that society should treat all men (if not women) as responsible adults, fit to be given a basic education and a vote, it was all the worse to have to deal with some people who were clearly neither responsible nor fit.

There were clearly different forms and degrees of unfitness. There were those who were simple, and every village expected to have its idiot, wandering amiably and harmlessly around. Then there were others who went mad. They could go mad in different ways. For generations one of the commonest forms of mild derangement had been named as melancholy. That name itself – meaning suffering from an excess of black bile – dated from the time before William Hervey had discovered the circulation of the blood (in 1628), and rested on the ancient notion that our bodies are made up of four humours – blood, phlegm, bile and black bile – and that perfect health rests upon a balance between the four. Other forms of madness were also recognized. Somebody who suddenly behaved wildly and howled might be rabid, having been bitten by a dog with rabies (or *la rage*, as the French call it). For medicine a breakthrough came when Pasteur discovered how to inoculate patients against rabies by giving them a small injection of the contamination.

That breakthrough led physicians to see that at least some forms of madness could be clinically treated. If some could be, then it was only a matter of time and patient research before medicine extended its frontiers. Then madness, instead of being an irrational and frightening phenomenon that mocked all human pretensions, could be corralled and subdued. Some of its edges might remain untameable. For those born mentally subnormal – a phrase that began to come into medical use towards the end of the nineteenth century – there was probably little that doctors could do, any more than they could make good some major physical defect at birth. But since human beings could be prevented from attacks of rabies by the same means as they could be protected from other merely physical diseases, then madness began to lose its terror.

Meanwhile the study of hypnosis was moving from the fairground into the fringes of respectable medicine. Making patients relax to the point where they would say things that they were normally afraid to admit pointed the way towards an understanding of the workings of the human mind that could respond to analysis and so to treatment.

The next phase of development brought together the advances of clinical medicine and the work of psychologists. The name of Sigmund Freud towers over the science of psychiatry, the study of the healing of the human mind. While psychiatrists placed their patients on a couch, rather than an operating table, their method was intended to be as scientific as that of the work of physicians. They wrote up their cases, and in learned journals discussed their analysis and treatment in the same way as specialists in physical disease discussed theirs. With growing confidence, the idea grew that psychological disorders were as capable of diagnosis and cure as physical maladies were.

This general understanding has long since become commonly accepted. We live in a society where one in five of us expects at some time or another to be treated for mental illness. Mental handicap, too, in its various forms, is no longer as frightening a phenomenon as it was for so long, because now we suppose that we understand something about its causes and how to help those who are afflicted to make the most of their limited capabilities.

Allowing that mental handicap has its own corner, what most of us stand to catch is some form of mental illness. Simply to put it like that does take much of the sting out of it. If we have not been patients ourselves, almost all of us must know somebody who has been in mental hospital for a spell of treatment. There they are, amongst us once more, no longer locked away for ever. If anything, they wear their scars with pride. It is no longer shameful to admit to having been an in-patient, but rather ex-patients like to talk about their treatment as a matter of general interest. They like to think that they can expect sympathy when they talk of their nervous breakdown, and the stress that led them to make their temporary withdrawal from the battlefield of life. For they can assume that whoever they talk to has similar symptoms, and that nobody can expect to go through life unscathed.

Margaret certainly liked to trade on her periods in hospital. There she was, indefatigable secretary of the local branch of the Mothers' Union, but every so often things got too much for her and she had to go in for another spell of treatment. Out of Christian compassion, the other members of the branch did their best to go along with her heroics. A wise vicar's wife recognized how much it meant to Margaret to be able to resume her labours with the branch correspondence whenever she came back home, and so the other members jollied her along. Though they found her tedious enough, and could only take her in small doses, they saw that she could manage the work, and what important therapy it was for her.

Then there is Alec. He has long made his name as an entertainer, and those who go to see him perform on stage take all his exuberance as part of his act. They have no idea that he has had several spells in mental hospital, and convalescence in various rest homes. Thanks to a zealous agent, and his own ability to go on giving his performances, Alec turns his mental instability into his stock in trade.

For Alec is a manic-depressive, so labelled by the doctors who treat him. Anybody who has to work closely with him finds it a very wearing process. For a time he will have boundless energy, and then it is at first exhilarating and soon maddening to try to keep up with him. When others are tired after a long day's rehearsal, he will be all for having just one more go. Then a week later, he does not come to rehearsal. There is a phone call to mumble some excuse, followed the day after by a long illegible letter, scrawled and counter-scrawled with explanations for his failure to arrive. These pages are full of apology, full of self-pity. Alec is in one of his depressive phases.

Douglas is another. Three years in a Japanese prisoner-of-war camp have always provided a ready explanation for his ups and downs of mood. In all his years as a successful journalist, those who worked with him learned to be wary of him. His moods became more and more extreme, and the little pills that he produced from his waistcoat pocket seemed to do nothing to control them. Then he had a serious accident, assuming that it was an accident, that forced him into early retirement. Now in premature old age, he sits in his room and can scarcely bear any human contact.

Anybody will know their Margaret, their Alec, their Douglas, and be able to fill in the details of such case histories. There are marriages that have been less than totally happy, and how many people can claim to have totally happy ones? There are problems with the children, but then any parents should expect to have problems with their children. There are financial worries – there are always financial worries, as most us live up to the hilt and beyond our incomes. There are frustrations at work, that are as much to be expected as the weather. There is the constant friction of hanging on to life and making sense of it.

That much, with minor variations, is the experience of us all. Yet four out of five of us can expect to get through life without a spell in mental hospital, without acquiring a psychiatric label. Four out of five of us are not going to be registered as manic-depressive, or with any of the other labels that turn people into psychiatric cases.

Some of these labels, clearly, describe extreme deviations in behaviour and imbalances in the mind. The inmates of Broadmoor or Rampton have been diagnosed by society as unfit for everyday intercourse, and locked away. To name them as psychopaths or as severely schizoid gives the rest of us an assurance that experts have examined them, and been able to describe what is wrong with them. Thus we can sleep of nights, in the confident belief that there is sufficient knowledge around to pin a long descriptive name upon those who offend against the canons of behaviour. We can presume, too, that in such prisons psychiatrists continue their examination and treatment, and do their best, by means of drugs or some other therapy, to make their patients better.

It is in middle age that loneliness acquires this new face. It is not so much now that we are lonely in an unfamiliar world. Ours is not the loneliness of the teenager, asking the question "Who am I?" It is not that of the young adult, coming to terms with life alone. It is not even quite the same as it was for us a few years earlier, faced with blows to our self-esteem and the frailty of the world that we had been busy creating for ourselves. By middle age, loneliness has stripped these guises, and comes at us unmistakeable.

What has till now been unfamiliar becomes strange. The enthusiasms of younger people no longer command our attention. If when younger, we threw ourselves into causes, now the excitement has gone out of them. Many middle-aged people pursue the causes of their youth with doggedness. They are members of the committee, and there is this work to be done and that. They may remain dedicated to the cause, whether it is a political party or simply running the local boys' football club. But now it is a matter of simply carrying on, because the job needs to be done, and who else has the same experience and commitment?

This disenchantment passes as a sign of maturity. The youth club leader who is approaching the age of fifty, and still insists on being as hearty as ever, is something of a figure of fun. He has not grown up. The woman in her forties who dresses as she did twenty years ago is equally to be pitied. She is refusing to admit her age, and takes nobody in but herself. In not adjusting to the passing years, people in middle age risk cutting themselves off from the reality of life around them and then it may well be that loneliness catches them unawares. For others do not take kindly to those who live on the illusions of the past. They come to regard them as eccentrics, as a little bit crazy, even. So such people find themselves left behind on the beach as the tide ebbs, and it is a lonely place to be.

The hard world of today beaches others in middle age. The craft worker laid off after thirty years, pressed into taking his redundancy money, does not find it easy to get a decent new job that will give him anything like the satisfaction that he has till now unthinkingly enjoyed. The office executive is in a similar plight. Local newspapers like to report cases of men who could not bear to tell their wives that they had lost their jobs, and so set off daily with their briefcases on a journey to nowhere until their security pay ran out.

Women in senior positions may be at less risk. They have pursued their careers to this point, and made their mark in what remains a predominantly masculine world. It is easier for personnel officers to pick off surplus men than it is to throw out women, whose contribution to the firm's life is in any case probably more substantial. Yet when Elizabeth's job in a public relations company folded under her, she never recovered. For two years she was unemployed. By the time she did manage to find a new job, it was not such a good one, nor so interesting, as the one she had had before. She found herself working for a much younger boss, and her work was not as good as it should have been. Within six months she was once more out of work, and this time it was for ever. She did her best to make light of her problems, but they gnawed at her, and gradually even her small circle of friends could not bear to visit her any more. It would have been easier if she had been ready to admit her misery in defeat. Somehow such honesty was beyond her, and when her friends found their offers of sympathy rejected, their wells soon dried. Elizabeth became an intensely lonely person, only too likely to drink and smoke herself to a premature death.

Peggy was a more extreme case. Somehow a benevolent institution had kept her on its payroll for twenty years, with one department after another being coaxed to find a space for her. She was drinking, to steel herself for the journey home to her bedsit. Every trick in the disciplinary book was played to try to help her reform. Eventually the time came when there was nothing for it but to enforce her early retirement on grounds of health. For some months her long-suffering office colleagues appeased their conscience about her by going to call. There would be a clink of bottles being hidden before she answered her door, and she would open it with a bright smile and a ready embrace. Even Peggy could never admit to being lonely, though her stories of all her activities and the people she met grew more and more fanciful. Then the inevitable happened: her landlord threw her out. Now, they say, Peggy is to be found, sleeping rough, around Clapham Junction. Occasionally she will telephone the office, to talk to some former colleague, to say she will be late in today. It is the classic cry for help, but anyone who tries to meet her at the time and place she suggests never finds her. She may be dead by now.

Years previously, her doctors had despaired of Peggy. Several times they tried to dry her out, or put her on some pill that would not go with alcohol. She even had a spell in hospital, but that was simply because she fell over and broke her leg. To say, "If only her doctors had diagnosed her as lonely long before" is to admit the fragility of such a diagnosis. Everybody knew that Peggy was lonely, for all that she put such a brave face on it, and at her best was the life and soul of the party.

Moreover, Peggy was a Roman Catholic, with strong memories of her Catholic upbringing in Lancashire. She had long stopped practising, but at one point a Catholic colleague of hers did persuade her to go to confession, and primed a priest friend of his on Peggy's situation. For Peggy, even that provided only a respite. She claimed, for a few weeks afterwards, to be going to Mass every Sunday, and even talked with pride of her new jobs in the parish. A few months later, and all that was forgotten.

For several decades, there have been intermittent attempts to see the work of general practitioners and ministers of religion as complementary. The late Rev. Dr Gilbert Russell was a pioneer of this endeavour. Himself a practising psychiatrist, he looked for ways of making good the traditional duet of the doctor with his care of the body and the priest with his care of the soul. Such bodies as the Churches' Council for Health and Healing have done their best to foster this link. Within the mainstream traditions of Christianity, too, there have been various enterprises to encourage the churches to make more of their gift of healing. Within the Roman Catholic Church, Lourdes is only the best-known example of a shrine dedicated to healing.

Under the long pressure of rationalism, the protestant tradition let go of any belief that it was empowered to heal, until Christian Science emerged around the beginning of this century with fresh promise of divine healing. Its emergence prodded sensitive people within the main protestant streams to reflect on their abandonment of this ministry, and from the early years of this century such bodies as the Church of England Guild of St Raphael came into being to explore once more Jesus's command to his followers to heal the sick. Clearly superstition and magic were suspect, but the use of prayer and the ancient rite of anointing could touch those with faith. While there are always wilder sects and individuals with a healing gift who make preposterous claims, and feed upon the gullibility of the crowds that they collect, the quieter approach of sober Christians does touch springs that medical training neglects.

For medical training is still dominated by the view that its business is with the body. The mind is an annexe for post-graduate specialists, and how can medicine locate the soul? Against this pragmatic approach to healing, the churches modestly point to their own understanding of human beings. The conventional division of body, mind and spirit may not serve, but the biblical picture of the whole man, a body with breath, is proving hardier.

Though the techniques may be more sophisticated, that threefold picture of medicine is as inadequate as the classical picture of the four humours. Whatever terms we use, whatever artificial divisions we impose as specialists stake their claims, any approach to medicine that denies the wholeness of the person is unsatisfactory.

It is by seeing the person as a whole that loneliness comes into its own. It does not fit into the GP's stock list of complaints. For a physician to diagnose somebody as lonely goes beyond the professional brief. Yet time and again doctors must recognize that this is what is wrong with their patients. They may talk of headaches, of not feeling themselves, and only expect a little reassurance and some pills. They might be deeply offended if the doctor told them that they were suffering from loneliness. Afterwards they might be relieved, knowing that someone had told them the truth. But just as doctors avoid telling cancer patients what is really wrong with them, because it sounds like a death knell, so they consider it none of their business to pronounce a patient as lonely. For loneliness too sounds as if it is beyond the power of any doctor to cure.

For many the psychiatrist is the qualified replacement for the minister of religion. Psychiatrists are trained to understand the human mind, and have the skills to hasten its cure. Against them, what has the minister of religion to offer to somebody who is basically sceptical of the premises upon which he works? One answer may simply be his accumulated expertise. Not every vicar, let alone inexperienced young curate, can pretend that his studies have given him an insight into other people's souls. Yet years of experience in dealing with people should lead to a professional wisdom that the doctor does not expect to acquire. A minister of religion does become used to dealing with people in distress. He hears their confessions of sin, and the expression of guilt that goes with it; he spends time with them as they lie dying, and thereafter makes it his business to comfort the bereaved. Particularly as he prepares people for marriage, or for the baptism of their infants, he makes it his business to become intimate even with those whose church connection is slender. All in all a Christian pastor, or any other minister of religion who has a flock to mind, is a specialist in human unease, and in the loneliness which so often lies at its root.

Beyond that, within the churches, there are those who specialize in counselling. Men and women, ordained or lay, their gift and their training lies in coping with people's muddles and miseries. They may often want to refer such people through their GP to a psychiatrist, recognizing that there is a medical aspect to their disorder. Equally they can tell when referral to a doctor is not the answer, and their own skills and experience are more appropriate. They may well be far better than physicians at getting those in their care to face the roots of their own distress. Since their profession hangs upon trying to bring people into some sort of healing relationship with divine power, they need not hesitate, as GPs do, to enquire into loneliness.

When they do that, they can bring their faith into play. A minister of religion's business is to purvey his or her own belief that there is a divine power, available to us all, ready to release as much life into us as we are open to receive. This belief in a holy source of strength outside ourselves, full of all the goodness that there is, challenges the self-pity upon which loneliness feeds. No wise minister of religion is going to pretend that this power is instantly on tap to effect immediate and total release from the misery of loneliness. Nor is he going to pretend that an individual's faith in that power automatically cures loneliness. Some of the most devout saints have wrestled a lifetime with loneliness and self-doubt. But the least that a Christian minister can do is to remind the lonely person that in the garden of Gethsemane Jesus experienced loneliness to the full. Even in the deepest pit of loneliness the person who owns some faith in Christ has the comfort of knowing that he is not alone. In the person of Jesus, the God who makes us all has drunk the cup of loneliness to the dregs.

6.

Under the Lonely Sky

Somebody wrote to the Independent Broadcasting Authority complaining that an advertisement for British Rail's steamers on Lake Windermere was misleading. It quoted Wordsworth's line: "I wandered lonely as a cloud" and the complaint was that the daffodils which delighted the poet were not there but by Ullswater. The complaint was rejected, the IBA considering that it was very unlikely that people would be rushed into going to the wrong lake.

We have been conditioned into thinking of loneliness as a demon stalking in the wilderness of bricks and mortar. The solitary bedsit, the echoing street, alien figures in a crowd, are all props of the lonely urban stage. By contrast we are tempted to assume that in the countryside there is little room for loneliness. Day by day *The Archers* offers its millions of listeners a saga of country life. For all the ups and downs of living in and around Ambridge, there is a feeling that everybody knows everybody, and that a shawl of care warms even the oddest characters.

The enduring popularity of *The Archers* suggests that we want this reassurance that the countryside is kindly. Something of the same appeal comes across in Yorkshire Television's serial *Emmerdale Farm*. There we watch stories played out against the rhythm of the seasons, and human life is to scale. Serials in urban settings lack that perspective. In *Coronation Street* what glimpses we have of the sky are of a uniform grey; in *Crossroads* we are rarely outdoors; the pace of *Eastenders* is set by events, while even on that Liverpool suburban estate where they film *Brookside*, the weather only matters when somebody wants to wash their car.

Most of us live in towns and cities, and hanker for the countryside. There, we like to imagine, it is easy to belong, and people can live out their lives in a far more natural way. It is an enduring fancy, but it has very little substance in it. Those who make careful studies of rural life today recognize that it is in practice "suburbia with more trees".

The vicar of an idyllic village near Chester was showing a pair of students something of the realities of life in his parish. His main point was how little it contains its parishioners. Only the very young and the dwindling number of very old people who still live at home pass their days within its bounds. By the age of nine children are away in the bus to the Middle School in another village, and by thirteen are taking the longer ride to school in the city. After that the city strengthens its pull. Further education is there, most jobs are on its periphery. The supermarkets are there, sucking almost all the trade from the village shop, which is constantly threatening to close. Anybody who needs anything done in their homes has to look for services from the city. That is where all the public offices are, and all the everyday business of life centres around it. So the idyllic village is little more than a dormitory, and it is an uphill task for the few stalwarts to maintain any resemblance of village life.

Ronald Blyth's *Akenfield*, portrait in film and print of a village in Suffolk, painted a similar picture in fine detail. The overall picture it gave was that those who live in a village see themselves as second-class citizens in a society that is geared to urban living. Public transport declines, and it is harder to maintain choirs and cricket and football clubs. The young men whose fathers and great-uncles were happy to turn out on a Saturday for the squire's eleven are now off on their bikes about their own affairs.

Villages are not the close-knit communities that they once

were, and there are fewer extended families than there used to be to serve as the mortar of village life. When there is a family event – a christening, a wedding, a funeral – cousins have to be summoned from miles away, and stand awkwardly at reception parties wondering who they know.

Particularly in her novels based on Miss Marple, Agatha Christie caught something of the sinister loneliness of village life. Behind the trim front gardens and the freshly painted mullion window-frames, who could tell what lonely secrets lurked? Edith and Mabel and Ethel are three elderly relations, Edith widowed, the other two never married, who continue to live their separate lives a few doors away from one another in a small country town. In a previous generation they might very well have moved in together, as their three old aunts once had. These three have the means to live their own lives, apparently self-contained and sufficient. The two old maids find their fulfilment in their church commitments, wondering who will take over when they can no longer manage. Edith has never been "church", and though her son comes faithfully to see her every week, life for her has never been the same since she lost her husband. She is the only one who admits to being lonely. "I think the others are, too," she says, "but they will never admit it."

"So many village people are lonely", says Edith. "It is so quiet, and nothing ever happens. Since the factory closed, what is there to do here? The men go to work in the towns – if they are lucky enough to have a job. Apart from the few who work in the shops, there is no work for the women. The spirit has gone out of the place. We are all living a slow death. Whatever you do, don't come and live here. There is nothing to belong to any longer and you would die of loneliness, as the rest of us are doing."

Edith exaggerates, looking back on her long life in the place, with its fading store of happy memories. But there is much to support what she says. Many of the cottages are up for sale, as those who have tried rural life for a few years find that they cannot adapt to it. Brian and Mary are one such couple. They had moved out, full of hope, and talked of establishing their own little business. That had come to nothing, and Brian took a job in a town ten miles away. "It has been tearing us apart", Mary admits. "I get so lonely I could scream. Sometimes I have thought of walking out on him, but what about the children and where would I go? Then I realize that it is living here which makes me so lonely. I feel I don't belong. We have been here five years. At first everybody seemed friendly enough, but – I don't know – somehow I just can't fit in. We shall have to move back nearer London. I feel at home there. This place gives me the creeps."

Edith's son Roger is an estate agent. He can tell the same story several times over. Business stays brisk because people cannot settle. As he sees it, they all seem to be chasing their own tails. "Yes, you could say they were all lonely, as Mother says. But there are different kinds of loneliness. The young ones are too worried to be lonely, and they think they have one another for support. But I hear it all. *She* takes me upstairs and tells me that she has never felt at home here; it is all his place. *He* shows me round his workshop and complains that she takes no interest in all his efforts. Then you get the middle-aged ones, surprising how many of them are on their own. They are always looking for somewhere where they can start again. It has to be just right. You can always tell if they are serious, or if they are just pretending and wasting our time. With those ones, we take them off our mailing lists pretty sharpish. Very few of them bother to put themselves back on. They were just househunting for a hobby. Sometimes I say, 'Don't forget that you have to bring yourself with you'. They give me a funny look when I say that. It is as if they were trying to run away from themselves, the women especially."

Survivor of two failed marriages, and the children by his

first wife now grown up and gone away, Roger has his own views on loneliness. "In the end you have to learn to live with yourself. It is hard enough trying to live with somebody else, and I haven't done very well at that. Living with myself is even harder. I'm always wanting to say 'Oh dammit!' and shut off the world. The work keeps me going of course, but inside myself I keep bumping into my shadow. At my age there is no point in moving into a city – I've lived all my life in the country. But then I look at Mother and I think, now she really is lonely. What have I got to grumble about?"

At the beginning of this century some twenty per cent of the working population worked on the land. A generation ago mechanization had brought that figure down to eight per cent. Now it is three per cent. Big farms, and modern machinery have demobbed the armies of landworkers. Country life has lost its rationale, and it has also lost much of its scaffolding. The village school, the doctor and the parson are no longer there to give shape and self-sufficiency to it all. The big house has been taken over by some company as a training unit, or sold to Arabs who take no interest in village life. Where there is no longer a strong sense of common purpose, it is very easy for people to feel lonely.

Villages rally to a crisis. When there is the threat of an unwanted development, such as a dump for nuclear waste or a major airport, the villagers rush to defend themselves. A hundred or more people find the time to stand in the way of the contractors' lorries. Even those who thought themselves isolated will become involved. At the very least they will be glad to sign a petition, or they may come out of their shells and reveal some unexpected talent to be used in the common defence. Over a cup of tea in the village hall, barriers of mutual indifference tumble, as everybody discovers a common loyalty. That strange man from up the lane is ready to keep the books, the woman from Hill Cottage who never spoke to anybody turns out to be a dab hand at drawing sketch maps. Whoever said that village life was lonely?

It is the heady experience of wartime all over again, when everybody lent a hand to help fill sandbags, or cheerfully paraded to be fitted for their gas masks. The adrenalin begins to run, and there is something for everybody to do. There is no time now to feel lonely.

For the loneliness of country life is the loneliness of boredom. There are those acres of time to be filled, and not enough to fill it with. Looking after a garden, keeping a house spruce, may occupy many hours, may bring its own private satisfactions. The horticultural show and the church fete do what they can to put a gloss of shared achievement upon these humdrum activities. Yet for many individuals these joint efforts ring hollow. The usual busy people run them, and Mrs So-and-So's jam and old Mr Whatnot's chrysanthemums will win the prizes as they always do. It is small comfort to enter pots of also-ran marmalade or inferior blooms. For all the goodwill that village events are meant to generate, as a by-product of raising money for the church tower fund, they only underline the loneliness of those who feel themselves to be lonely.

The countryside has witnessed many experiments to combat loneliness. Ebenezer Howard's garden cities at Letchworth and Welwyn early in this century set out the ideal of communal living in a country setting. Nearby, in Cambridgeshire, the Village Colleges established between the wars proclaimed that continuing education was the birthright of all. Still a unique enterprise, village colleges continue to meet a demand, and challenge the wide skies of the fens. Dotted elsewhere around the English countryside are numbers of adult educational institutions of one sort or another that offer short residential courses on a wide range of subjects. Mainly these are public undertakings, but one of the most successful is a private venture: the college in the Old

Rectory at Fittleworth in Sussex, run as a family enterprise. To attend a course there is to come across a wide mix of people, many of them living on their own, who in this setting find intellectual stimulus and company. Many of those on courses are regulars, prepared to learn anything from archaeology to brass-rubbing. They make no secret of the fact that they go on coming because they are lonely on their own at home; but they do not come just for the company. What they learn matters too. Graham Salmon, who runs it, reckons that the chief value of the college is that it does provide an atmosphere in which lonely people can come to learn something without letting their guard down further than they intend.

These are only a few examples of so many varied educational enterprises that all over the countryside appeal to those who want to be taken out of themselves and learn something fresh. To mention them risks falling into the category of brisk advice: "Go out and embrace the world!" For anyone with any experience of adult education colleges knows only too well that large numbers of the students are there primarily to get away from their sense of loneliness. To enrol for the first time, and take the step of walking into a classroom full of strangers, is not easy for those who are deeply lonely. They cannot hang their loneliness up on a peg in the cloakroom, or pretend to a buoyancy that they do not feel.

Such lonely people might do better if they could admit their sense of loneliness to one another. In an adult class that stays together, and defies the threats of closure as its numbers shrink, those who first came as nervous individuals can achieve a sense of mutual support. It is a miniature village rallying to face a crisis.

Education centres are not the only places in the country-side that set out to meet the needs of lonely people. Scattered all over the country are religious houses of one kind or another that are ready to open their doors to those who may be glad to find a haven in them. Their particular appeal varies widely, and those who might feel at ease in one place would shy away from another. The house that proclaims in its vestibule "JESUS LOVES YOU – NO SMOKING" defines its clientele, and repels strangers.

Religious houses set in the countryside follow the very old tradition that led those who wanted to get nearer to God to take themselves off into the desert. The lushness of the English landscape may not offer the austerity of the wilderness, but at least it is away from crowds and noise and all the distractions of urban life. So those who go into retreat in such places go to confront their own essential loneliness in a setting where there is little to cover it.

Anyone who has never been on retreat may be daunted by the prospect. They may very well think that they would suffocate in such very religious surroundings. In fact many of the houses that invite people to make private retreats under their roof, especially those run by sisters, are models of unobtrusive welcome. A visitor need say nothing to anybody, and can spend a few days alone and silent, at least sure of regular meals and a comfortable bed. When the silence becomes unbearable, there are books, a garden to sit in or the countryside inviting a walk. In one room there is usually a record player, and a selection of soothing classics with which to break the silence.

For those who scream at their own loneliness, a few days in retreat might prove a very healing experience. There is the comfort of knowing that those who live in the house have spent their time learning to confront their own loneliness. The lovely ideal of the religious life is that it provides a frame in which the individual becomes part of a community dedicated to the praise and the service of God. For anyone to whom this ideal makes no sense, it is tempting to imagine the religious life as a life of self-delusion and self-indulgent withdrawal from the pain and misery of the everyday world.

Enough monks and nuns have written about their experiences to suggest otherwise. Even contemplatives, cut off from the world, reckon that they are close to its agonies. Without the clutter of detail, they can from their hearts sense enough of the misery to be able to lift it up in a steady flame of prayer. Those who write make it clear that for many of them it can be a satisfying and genuine way of life. For every Monica Baldwin or Karen Armstrong who has written about their escape from a mistaken calling, there is a Thomas Merton or a Harry Williams able to write with clarity and honesty about it. If some of Merton's writing, such as *Elected Silence*, is unbearably triumphant, Harry Williams in such books as *The True Wilderness* does touch the sore point of distress that we all feel with uncompromising precision.

"Our isolation is really us – inwardly without sight or hearing or taste or touch. But it doesn't seem like that. Oh no. I ask myself what I am isolated from, and the answer looks agonizingly easy enough. I am isolated from Betty whom I love desperately and who is just the sort of woman who could never love me. And so to feel love, I think, must at the same time be to feel rejection. Or I feel isolated from the social people who, if noise is the index of happiness, must be very happy indeed on Saturday evenings. Or I feel isolated from the competent people, the success-boys who manage to get themselves into print without getting themselves into court. Or I feel isolated, in some curious way, from my work. I find it dull and uninviting. It's meant – it used – to enliven me and wake me up. Now it deadens me and sends me to sleep. Not, in this case, because I'm lazy, or thinking of tomorrow's trip to London, but because it makes me feel even more alone. Or I feel isolated from things which once enchanted me, the music I play, the poetry I read, the politics I argue about. I go on doing it now as a matter of routine, not in order to be, but in order to forget, to cheat the clock. The L.P. record will take forty minutes if you play both sides, and then it will be time for tea" (Harry Williams, *The True Wilderness*, p. 30).

The L.P. that will take forty minutes if you play both sides dates this passage, and it was published in 1965 before Harry Williams left his comfortable life as a don at Cambridge and joined the Community of the Resurrection at Mirfield, on a windswept slope.

In that setting Harry Williams is one of thirty resident priest members of the Community who follow their hard calling under one rambling roof. Anyone who spends a little while as a guest at Mirfield has a chance to learn something about silence. It is a quiet house, with strict rules about not talking in the passages, and, like so many other religious houses, complete silence from after the evening office in the church until after breakfast next morning. Normally there is conversation at lunch and supper, and a parlour where guests can feel at ease. But a pall of quiet hangs over the house, and what a visitor notices is the smallness of the small talk with which the members of the Community engage their visitors and one another. The rule of the house used to warn against the dangers of too intimate friendships, and to an observer it feels that, out of their obedience to the rule, the Mirfield fathers have learned how to discipline themselves and keep their distance from other people. So they harbour what in that extract Harry Williams calls their isolation, their private sense of loneliness.

They do not run away from it. They know that putting on the L.P. or trying to find some other distraction is to cheat themselves. Only by burrowing right into that silence are they going to capture the mole of loneliness that lurks somewhere inside, and then perhaps have a chance of taming it. It is a lifetime's occupation, and the harder they try, the more they realize what a difficult task it is. Just when they think that they have caught it, and can now face the world entire, the animal has a way of slipping between their fingers and delving deeper into the interior.

Those who lead the religious life are ordinary men and women. It is a hard life, and the process of training and selection that leads to a lifetime's profession should weed out those who are not fitted for it. So anyone who attaches themselves to a religious community out of short-lived enthusiasm or misplaced piety is likely to be invited to go before taking final vows. For it is a life that commits its followers to a permanent quest for the roots of their own true being.

That is a quest which every one of us has somehow to pursue, if we are to become anywhere near the real self that we have it in us to be. Most of us manage to spend most of our lives dodging the pursuit. Or else we take what seems the more attractive route of looking for ourselves through our friendships and our loves. We can hardly help having dealings with other people; even the most limited regular link, such as our daily exchange with the newsagent when we buy our paper, can give us its small measure of feeling that we belong where we are. Those who feel themselves lonely deny that they have any friends, and may make nothing of even these small daily encounters. Yet they can provide the first bricks in any attempt to rebuild the house that we inhabit. The Mirfield fathers, indeed any others in the religious life, may have something to teach those who shrink from even such modest relationships as a friendly exchange with the newsagent. Do not expect more from anybody else than you are prepared to give. Be sure that you are not just trying to splurge yourself on somebody else. Remember that they may feel as wary as you are, and that underneath they too have to wrestle with their own loneliness.

When it comes to friendship, we invest more and we look for more in return. Those who are conscious of their own loneliness like constant toothache may be so hurt by a lifetime of rejection that they refuse to believe that they have any capacity for making friends and keeping them. Amongst the most pitiable are those lonely people in later life who try to make friends with children. Society is now so alert to those dangers that the child has only to run sobbing home, and the offender will end up in court, charged with a crime that was not even intended. To try to make friends with other adults is to risk one more rebuff, and children are the only way out.

Yet what is classically true for the best friendships of adolescence remains true for other friendships throughout life. Friendship stems naturally from facing the world together, rather than from looking into one another's eyes. To do things together, and find pleasure in it, is the staple of friendship. It may be something perfectly everyday, like decorating a room together. For a lonely person in a bedsit to invite the person from the next room in for a cup of tea may be awkward. To ask them in to hold the ladder is much easier.

Anyone who has ever been involved in a house-to-house collection will know something of this experience. To call on a stranger is always a risk. To call, as parsons reckon that they are entitled to do, simply to get to know somebody, is much riskier. The door may be immediately slammed, or there is the opposite risk of being invited in for an outpouring that goes on and on. In those situations the well-intentioned caller is wondering how to get away without making matters worse than they were before. In between these extremes, calling with a collecting tin is an easy thing to do. "They are always after your money" is the familiar complaint. Yet to call and invite a stranger to contribute to a well-known humanitarian cause breaks ice in a manageable way. Only a very few hard-hearted people refuse to give anything. Most people find it so much easier to fish for a few coppers from their purse or their pocket, if only to get rid of the caller with the least fuss and bother. That caller, of course, need not be a parson, immediately identifiable by a dog-collar. It can be anybody, whose identification is the collector's badge that the law of the land requires. It is a badge that immediately tells the person opening the front door that the visit is limited and honourable.

In these doorstep encounters lie the seeds of friendship. For here are two strangers brought together by a common cause. The little act of holding out a tin, and of putting money into it, means that they do not have to look at one another too openly. This is not the beginning of an acquaintance that might go further than one or the other wants. It is a small self-contained exchange that need go no further. In practice, it often can lead to something more. The person at the front door can say how pleased they are to be called upon; the caller can truthfully say that there is no time now to prolong the conversation, but can make a date to call again. By the time of the second visit, both parties know a little of what to expect of one another, and the relationship can go on from there.

To go collecting from house-to-house, or to go canvassing for a political party, is not easy for shy people to do. They prefer to sit at home addressing envelopes. For walking from house to strange house, under the open sky, calls for a certain confidence in the cause. The caller depends upon the goodwill of those who answer the doorbell or the knocker. You stand on the doorstep, preparing yourself for one more unknown response. It may be raining, and the evening is drawing on. You might have a colleague, doing the same business somewhere up the road, and there is comfort in the thought that there are others about, somewhere, collecting for the same cause. Even so you are on your own, at the mercy of the elements, and of the person whom you are about to meet.

Standing on that doorstep beside you is loneliness. For this moment captures all the isolation that any of us may feel as we brace ourselves for the next encounter. Each one of us is in effect all the time under that sky, and it is raining and it is beginning to get dark. It is tempting to call it a day, and make tracks for our own private place. We all, in the end, want to run for cover in the secrecy of our own loneliness. Yet there we stand, waiting for somebody else to unbolt the door, because that is how the world gets on with its business. However lonely we feel, as from their immense distance the first stars show, we are part of this world, and there is a place for each one of us in it somewhere, and our job of work to be done.

In St Paul's Cathedral hangs Holman Hunt's famous picture "Behold I stand at the door and knock". There is no doorhandle, and there are thorns growing up around the doorpost. The white figure of Christ with his lantern stands under the brooding sky, waiting for a response. The picture has inspired many sermons, for its message is plain and poignant. For those who find it hard to receive, the thought that each one of us stands in the same position may bring some light. None of us can effectively command the response of others. Those who try, by manipulating, by bullying, or simply by looking hangdog, cannot expect an open reply to their knocking. The figure in the picture stands patiently, as we have to learn to stand. At least then we are making no unreasonable demands when the door is unlocked to greet us.

7.

The Valley of the Shadow

It is a constant surprise to find how many people are well into their forties before they have ever attended a funeral. Years ago they lost their grandparents, but then it was thought not nice for a youngster to have to attend such a gloomy event, and to see the unyielding process of dispatch as the coffin slides along its rails or (less frequently) is lowered into the grave.

Indeed, those whose elderly parent has just died are almost offended at the suggestion that they might want to bring their own children to the funeral. "Oh, he's only a nipper", says Dad. "It wouldn't be fair." "But was he close to his Gran?" "Yeah, I suppose he was." "Then why not ask him if he would like to come?" So a grieving grandchild does attend, and may well be the only member of a dumbstruck family gathering to go up to the unknown clergyman afterwards and say thank you.

Beyond the age of fifty, and certainly by sixty, death becomes a familiar companion. There may be aunts and uncles left, still marvellously together, or tucked away into the security of homes for the elderly, but for people around retirement age it is their contemporaries who are careless enough to die. "And he was only sixty-one", they say indignantly, as if it was selfish of him to leave them in the lurch like this.

To lose a friend or a colleague by death is a grief. To lose a brother or sister, or someone else very close, is more of a loss. For then there is a lifetime to mourn, and all the painful thoughts of a flawed relationship getting in the way of happy memories. Worst of all is the loss of a husband or a wife. With that may well go long weeks or months of illness, nursing them, or visiting them in hospital, and at each visit wondering how many more there will be.

There has been much written in recent years on the subject of people dying, and those whose business is to look after them have developed a vocabulary of the stages by which death approaches. They may therefore be able to help the dying work their way through these successive stages, and give some advice to those near to them on how to conduct themselves. After the person has died comes the time for bereavement counselling, and for all who can to play their part in consoling the bereaved.

In England, it is an art that we largely have to learn from scratch. The rituals by which people make public their loss have largely gone. The heavy Victorian drapes, the black-edged note-paper and the carefully graduated stages of mourning have disappeared. They remain only as a relic in the customs of the royal court. Even the black armband is a thing of the past, and all that we have left are maimed funeral rites. We do not even keep the coffin in the house, as they still do in Scotland.

However long expected, death comes as a shock, and for those who are left the first few days demand a series of unfamiliar actions. The central one is arranging the funeral, and for many people the easiest thing is to contact the undertakers and leave the details to them. They know how to cope with it all, they will find a minister and get the whole wretched business dealt with as painlessly as possible. Most people in the first shock of bereavement never consider that they might have a hand in shaping the funeral service, so that it honours the dead person as well as possible, and does all it can to provide them with a satisfactory expression of their final farewells. So they are ready to make do with a reach-me-down funeral, and get it over and done with. An unknown minister may do his best to express his faith in the richer life beyond this one, but it is not easy to find words that transmit such conviction to a gathering of strangers, for whom it is all pie in the sky.

Without the comfort of a proper funeral, the first stab of grief is left bleeding, and it is then all the harder to begin the very slow process of healing that follows over the coming weeks and months and years. Even at the reception which as a rule follows a funeral, people are scarcely able to mention the dead person's name, or discuss what has brought them together. A handshake with the next-of-kin, and then over a glass of port or whatever is provided they find some relation whom they have not seen since the last such occasion, and fall into conversation about anything except the dead person. Anybody who does try to talk on that subject is considered embarrassing. So pocket handkerchiefs wipe away tears before they have a chance to flow, and the accepted behaviour is to carry on as if nothing had happened.

As if nothing had happened! With no tailor-made funeral, with no wake such as the Irish have to cover death with a mantle of hilarity, bereaved people in England have to learn to mourn alone. For a few days after the funeral there is the consoling business, perhaps, of writing to thank those who have sent floral tributes. After that, there is only the gaping hole; and for older people especially, only loneliness to fill it. For a few weeks acquaintances may stop in the street to say how sorry they are to hear the news, but after that the bereaved spouse is expected to get over the grief as quickly as possible, and not burden other people with it.

For what is there anybody else can say? Deeply religious people can find comfort in the assurance that their beloved is now in heaven, but the belief lost much of its power once the Church stopped preaching hellfire as a statistically more likely alternative. For bereaved people, it is hard enough coming to terms with the fact that their beloved is dead.

There are means of consolation open to them. They can display photographs of the dead person, play tapes of the beloved voice and – what so many widowed people find healing – through gardening have a sense that all is not lost. Favourite plants and flowers, in their annual cycle, are the most natural souvenirs of mortality and hope.

The stages of grief are now well documented. The shock of bereavement, however long expected, is so numbing that at first widowed people are often surprisingly high. A sense of elation carries them through the funeral and their immediate weeks of loss. Previously every day of their lives together had been something of a gamble. However long and confident their bond, each day was a new one, carrying the risk of something that could fray it. Come the death of one partner, and the uncertainty of all those years is over. The gamble has paid off, and like a life insurance policy that pays up when one of them dies, so comes an unexpected bonus of thankfulness. There is grief indeed, but it is draped in this coverlet of gratitude.

Then comes a spell when the widowed person can hardly believe their loss. They imagine that they can hear the familiar footsteps, or catch an echo of their late partner's voice. It may take months before they can learn to talk of "I" and they are apt to go on talking of their partner in the present tense.

During this second stage of grief, they may still enjoy the sympathy of friends and neighbours. For all that we have let go the paraphernalia of mourning, in England we are still for a time ready to show tenderness towards our grieving neighbours. It shows in gestures and actions rather than in speeches. The extra warmth of greeting in the street, a knock at the door to see if there is anything we can do, are amongst the shy ways by which we go on expressing our condolences.

This special tenderness can only be expected to last for a certain period. Death, after all, comes to everyone, and there is an unspoken limit to our tolerance of others' grief. The brisk lady who after six months said, "I have done my mourning now" and then became engaged to her childhood sweetheart well reflected common conventions. Beyond that, a year marks the span for the widowed to come through the worst of their grief. Once that anniversary has passed, then it seems reasonable to assume that they will have come to terms with their condition. Nothing can bring the loved one back, and we have to learn to feel at home with our loneliness.

"But I do go on being so lonely." Martha has outlived two husbands. She has no blood relatives, and in her mid-seventies finds it hard to regard the family bequeathed by her second husband, a retired vet, as anything to do with her. "I have nobody", is her constant cry, and nothing that these step-relations do can touch her sense of isolation.

Nor is Martha short of friends and neighbours. She has her own house, and in the cul-de-sac where she lives there is strong evidence of neighbourliness. She also has a number of women friends of her own age scattered around the country. They come for visits, and she goes to stay with them.

"But I am lonely." Martha's cry seems beyond comforting. Even five years after her second bereavement, she goes on saying it. It has become a kind of mantra for her. If the plea in these pages is, "Don't be afraid to say that you're lonely", then Martha fulfils it. She has little hesitation in saying that she is lonely to any of her circle who can bear to listen to her saying it yet once more.

Patience does wear thin. So many and varied attempts at sympathy seem to make no difference. Remind her how many friends she has, remind her of all her acts of kindness to those less fortunate than herself, and it makes no difference. It is no use telling her how fortunate she is to be in possession of all her faculties, or to be in her own home still. "But what if something happened to me," she wails, "if I fell downstairs and broke my leg?" So she talks of moving to sheltered accommodation but then turns down every practical possibility. "I should feel so lonely there." "But you feel lonely here!" "Ah, but it is home."

Martha explains her loneliness in terms of long empty evenings when nobody calls, nobody rings. She says that the house is too big for her, and haunts her with its memories. Meanwhile her natural dignity carries her through: she continues to dress well and care about her appearance; and she still gives up sherry for Lent. It is almost as if she had made a fetish of her loneliness. Being able to tell other people how lonely she feels, and so wring another word of sympathy out of them, is what keeps her going. Loneliness is her widow's weeds, that she dare not cast off.

Celia was widowed soon after celebrating her golden wedding. Her husband had a distinguished career in local government in the West Country, and Celia can look back on their marriage with pride and happiness. Her children are successfully married with children of their own, and Celia has no financial worries. What is more, she continues to lead a very active life, giving her valued services to this local charity and that; and when she is not busy with good works, she is always entertaining her lame ducks.

They readily admire Celia for the way she has coped with her bereavement. "Isn't she marvellous", is what they all say of her. It is a cliché, but it is one that seems quite appropriate. "And yet I am terribly, terribly lonely", she is ready to admit to those closest to her. "What's more, it gets worse." She brushes aside all protestations. "It is no use telling me I am not lonely, just because I am so 'marvellous'. I need to keep busy. That's all."

She has thought it all through very clearly. First, there is the desolation. She was very young when she married, Bertram several years older, so that all her life she knew that the likelihood was that she would outlive him. But she had given everything to make a success of her marriage. What she did on her own, like her work as a prison visitor and all those committees, came very much second. She had given her life to Bertram, and to their children because of him; and now he was gone. "And, yes, I am desolate; how can I be otherwise?"

Celia is not looking for easy words of consolation. They would come nowhere near touching the pangs of her loneliness. She is glad of just being able to be quiet in somebody else's company. She keeps her pride. A visitor may be plied with drinks; she just sips hers. The desolation is too private to do more than mention. Maybe somebody else can understand just a little of it, but it is hers, and not for sharing.

Beyond the desolation – this sense of total loss – lies the horror. Under the surface, the pit yawns. "It ought not to be like this", she protests. "Two years, three years, and now I should be over the worst. Bertram would be so ashamed of me." Is the horror then something to do with shame? By every canon, Celia is a very good woman, faithful to her husband's memory, brimming with kindness, and great fun. Yet to tax her with this generous assessment is to meet with a flat denial. "I am only conscious", she is inclined to say, "of how awful I am without him. He made me, and now look what I am!"

Celia is too appalled to be soft-soaped out of her misery. She has this picture of herself as a fraud, acting her part well enough, but underneath it all a fraud. That is what makes her so lonely: "I am on my own with myself, and I do not like it." It helps a little to suggest to Celia that this is more or less how we all feel. For Celia the horrid truth has only surfaced in the years since Bertram's death. Till then he sustained her, so that she did not have to think about it. Now he has gone and she is on her own – "really for the first time in my life".

It is as if, in her seventies, she is having to do a lot of living that she had never reckoned on having to do. All those fifty years and more, since she was a blushing young bride, she had never had to think who she was. Now, unkindly, when she is ill-equipped to face it, she has to learn to be herself. She names the experience as loneliness. It is an experience that far more people meet much sooner, and go on sparring with in the hope that it will soon be out for the count.

Jack has far longer to live with his grief. He was not much over fifty when his wife Ann died, after two years' struggle against cancer. Jack was a long-distance lorry driver, and because he was so often away, on Ann fell the main burden of bringing up their large family. When she fell ill, he did switch to a local haulage job, so as to be with her more. Now, with only their youngest daughter still at home, Jack describes his loneliness chiefly in terms of guilt. "I was never unfaithful, in the strict sense, but you know how it is. Sometimes I could have got home of a night, and stayed away instead. And there was a time – not so long ago, now, come to think of it – when we nearly split up. She said she couldn't stand me, I said, 'All right, get out, then'. 'No, you get out', she said, and it went on like that for several months. We still had three of the kids at home – no, wait, Lisa was already with Den – and I suppose that is what kept us together. For days we could hardly talk to one another."

Ann's death was a moving process. She died at home, with all her children around her, and Jack keeping constant watch. For ten days she lay on her death bed, it could be any moment now, and she was never alone. There was one night when they all expected her to go, and Jack sat there, bathing her forehead and holding her hand, murmuring of his love for her. In fact she fell into a coma, and lasted another three days. Afterwards Jack was totally exhausted, and at the funeral in church a week later was still in something of a daze.

With his youngest daughter's help, widowed Jack did all the sensible things. They redecorated the kitchen together, and did a lot of work in the garden which Ann had so much loved. They talked of moving house, but by the time a year was up that talk had come to nothing, and Jack had come to realize that he was better off to stay where he was. "I still feel that she is with me," he would say, "though I know perfectly well that she is not." Ann's church funeral had been for the sake of her own deep faith. Jack is a resolute agnostic. "Whatever you say," he likes to insist, "it really doesn't make any difference. She is dead, and that's it." He admits that he admired Ann's Christian convictions, and in some ways wished he shared them. "Even if I did, I should still feel lonely."

For though talking about the matter eases it for him, Jack cannot quite shake off this sense of guilt for the time when his marriage nearly failed. Then he laughs about it. "Now I wouldn't feel any better, would I, if I had this picture of her up there waiting for me armed with a rolling-pin?" As a widower, Jack is a very caring father and grandfather, but sees that as his own consolation. "It is no use telling me", he may say, "that this is how I make up for my guilty feelings. The two things don't have anything to do with one another, not the way I look at it. Being a kind Dad to the family, especially now that Ann's gone, isn't me being good. It's me being natural; just as I suppose you could say it was natural when I was trucking and did not always bother to come home for the night. That is how we are and we have to live with it."

Jack does not seem a prisoner of his own loneliness, as Martha does and Celia is. It makes a difference that he still has his youngest daughter at home; and it must make some difference that he is in his fifties, and not, as the two women are, approaching the age of eighty. Whatever faces they put on it, Martha and Celia know that they have only a coda of life to perform. At his age, Jack can look forward to a good long spell, time perhaps to accept his loneliness not as the dregs but as the medicine of his life. He says firmly that he has no intention of marrying again – "it is all too much hassle" – but you never know. Instead he sets himself the challenge of learning to live the rest of his life on his own, and that way coming to terms with his own loneliness.

For elderly people living on their own, and so at the mercy of loneliness, there are numbers of supports. One of the most important is pets. No doubt the market research of the petfood companies would reveal the proportion of such people who have a dog or a cat or at least a budgerigar. It so happened that soon after her second bereavement, Martha had to have her poodle put down. She had always had a poodle, and now to lose a husband and a dog one after the other redoubled her grief. She was frightened of having another dog – she was afraid that a pup might outlive her; but fortunately she was able to get one several years old, and so that became her companion.

For dogs are "man's best friend" and we can all think of people living on their own who are never without their dog. A dog that has grown up as a pet is the most loyal company. Their owners can treat them as confidantes, and they keep and respect those confidences. Appealing eyes and a tongue lolling to kiss it better are always at the ready. There is no criticism in that look, no reservation in the lick. Human companionship has so much more to offer and receive, but it always has its hidden flaws. The relationship between owner and dog, for all its limitations, can soothe away the fears of loneliness.

Anyone can be critical of the consolation that dog-owners find from their pets. There is something in the old observation that they grow to look like one another, and it is easy to talk of self-indulgence. A dog does not answer back, and so long as its owner looks after it, and befriends it, is well content. So the owner assuages any painful feelings of loneliness by pouring love into the four-footed friend. Being rejected by other people does not matter nearly so much when there is this bottomless repository of uncritical affection. Being ignored, being laughed at for this incestuous relationship, counts for little. From day to day a person with a good dog has no need to be afraid of feeling lonely. Underneath there may lurk a sense of utter loneliness. Used to the dog as a best friend, the owner may find it more and more difficult, and less and less worth bothering about, to make links with other people. The cartoons that we have of the solitary countryman with his lurcher, of the middle-aged woman on her own apart from her Alsatian, merge with the conventional picture of the greedy old lady with her lap-dog. All of them are at risk of hiding from themselves and the rest of the world, and becoming spitting images of their growling pet.

Dogs deserve most attention, because of their capacity for companionship. Cats are notoriously incapable of displaying the same affection; they can be stroked and made to purr, and they will cuddle up comfortably on anybody's lap. They are cold creatures, really. A pig makes a friendlier pet, and for one eleven-year-old girl who then kept one, her Wilberforce responded with intelligence and warmth. Other pets – the caged bird, the tortoise, the glossy fish in their tanks – may provide people who live on their own with another living creature to look at and care for; they are breakwaters against overwhelming isolation, but not much more.

For far more people living on their own, the most readily available hedge against isolation comes in over the air. BBC and IBA research indicates how much such people view and listen. Some years ago the IBA conducted an enquiry amongst elderly people who were living on their own. Its clearest finding was that such people treat television as "entertainment" but find radio "company". The obvious difference between the two media is that it is easy to listen to the radio and be doing something else at the same time. Television, though it often does not get it, invites more total attention. Beyond that the findings of this enquiry indicated that older people living alone felt more at home with radio.

It did not pry into their living rooms in the way that television seems to do. As one old lady put it, "I don't feel that I need to put my hat on in order to listen to the radio." She was not quite so naïve as the legendary old lady who used to wonder whether that nice Mr Bosanquet could see her when she was undressing, but evidently saw television as a visitor, who needed to be entertained if it was to be entertaining. Radio, on the other hand, she could listen to where she liked, in the bathroom, in the kitchen, in bed.

For elderly people living on their own, one constant fear is of having to go into a home. To be independent is a small price to pay for loneliness, and they know that once they are taken into geriatric care, they are in the crowded anteroom of death. Most old people's homes are not very companionable places. The staff will do their best to make sure that everybody is as comfortable as possible, but all too often the inmates are treated as bundles, to be jollied into conforming.

Marcia was whisked into such a place when she was ninety-one. There was nothing much wrong with her, as she put it, except old age. She was rather deaf, rather slow, but could manage on her own. But the warden of the sheltered accommodation where she lived was afraid that she might have an accident, and so they got her in. She had her own room, and a few of her bits and pieces around her, but for her it was simply not the same as being at home. "There's nothing to do here," she complained, "but eat and sit and sleep. The food's all right, and they mean well, but it is so boring." Marcia lived the year round before she did die; whatever they put on the death certificate, it was tempting to think that the real cause of her death was boredom.

For very old people find it extremely difficult to strike up new friendships with one another. It is all too exhausting; they are deaf and they are crotchety. So they sit round for hours in the rexine armchairs, in lines along four walls like a dentist's waiting room, nursing their private memories and their sense of loss. And they are bored.

Boredom is not identical with loneliness. Victor is an old soldier, almost totally paralysed. He can be dressed and got into a wheelchair, but he spends most of his day in his bedroom in a home. "I'm bored", he loves to say, challenging his visitor to deny it. "And are you lonely?" He reflects. "No, I'm not lonely. I am simply bored." "Are you afraid of the thought of dying?" "Not particularly – why should I be, eh?" "Do you wish you could die, then?" "No, not desperately … here, give me a turn." The price of visiting Victor is to be asked incessantly to move him into a more comfortable position. Apart from sucking a drink from a beaker, with his one good hand, there is nothing that he can do for himself. Yet he insists that he is not lonely. "I've got my thoughts, haven't I, I've got my memories. Why should I feel lonely? Tell you what, though. I'm always glad to see visitors, like seeing my daughter when she comes. I suppose knowing that they will come stops me feeling lonely, a bit. But I am always glad when they have gone. Funny that, isn't it, but that is how I feel. No, not lonely, just bored … here, turn me, will you?"

In the next room to Victor lived Edward, once upon a time a naval officer. He was acutely lonely. He had had two marriages, neither of them happy. For years he had spent his declining years in sheltered accommodation in Oxford, hopelessly trying to persuade the widowed housekeeper to marry him. Two young women undergraduates befriended him. At first he was puzzled why they should want to take up their time with an old man like him, but then his vanity came to the rescue, and he imagined that he kept them entertained by all his reminiscences of a colourful life. They did not mind him going on like that, but could never get him to appreciate that they valued him for himself. When he died, it was for one of them the first close experience of bereavement. She had grown very fond of Edward, and over the course of five years visited him faithfully, never making a fixed appointment week by week for fear of letting him down. Her greatest grief was that for all her years of affection, she had never succeeded in persuading him that there was no need for him to feel lonely now. In herself and her friend, if nobody else, he had two people who really did care about him, and would do so to the end.

8.

Don't Be Afraid to Say You're Lonely

"We have nothing to fear but fear itself." President F.D. Roosevelt's challenge to the USA at the height of the depression speaks well to all those who feel themselves to be lonely. For at bottom loneliness is fear; fear of other people, fear of oneself, fear of life.

The loneliest person I know is Cecil, and he is encased in fear. He is sorry for himself, of course, but it is no use saying "Snap out of it". As he delves into the bottomless pit of his misery, he can find nothing there but emptiness, and still the pit goes down. So he sits in a mental hospital, labelled depressive (with manic phases) and there seems to be no cure. Stooping like an old man (and he is scarcely fifty) he shuffles aimlessly up and down the corridors, beyond the reach of affection, however flawed. "I'm so afraid", is all that he can say, unable to describe the nameless fears that assault him.

He can list his problems easily enough. They are the usual catalogue – money, relations, and what is it all for anyway? He is even too afraid to commit suicide – somewhere a vengeful god might commit him to an eternity of banishment. So he stays trapped in his skin, and the doctors do not know what to do to help him. They are busy people, and take the only practical step – keeping him sedated at a level where he will comply and cause least nuisance. Who can blame them? They have other more hopeful patients on their books, and a long queue waiting for admission. They would love to discharge Cecil; he is there as a voluntary patient, and there are no clinical grounds for certifying him. But where could he go? He certainly could not go back to the house which he shared with his sister, until her untimely death. At the gathering after her funeral he flitted like a ghost, talking to nobody, scarcely able to answer a word when anybody tried talking to him, but stuffing himself with sandwiches in a corner.

Her will hoped that he might return home, though she was careful to bequeath the house elsewhere eventually. He would not be able to cope on his own. The bills and everything else would get totally on top of him. So for the moment Cecil remains trapped inside his body and the four walls of a mental hospital. His depression goes on and on; the manic phases are fewer and further in between. When he is high, he is ungovernable. He is a qualified nurse, he claims, he is owed pensions by all three armed services for his gallantry; Walter Mitty has nothing on him. Out he will go and run up ridiculous accounts: staying in hotels he cannot afford, ordering hi-fi equipment by mail order, all airs and swagger. With a few pounds in his pocket he will order drinks all round, and at the bar they nod and wink and are callous enough to accept his mad hospitality. Only the landlord stops them all buying Cecil one back. He has seen him in this state all too often, and wants no more trouble on his hands, thank you.

Cecil rushes off, his sister's complaisant terrier forging ahead on his lead. All these people in the street are their friends, then, aren't they? And Cecil will waylay Mrs So-and-So, asking eagerly how her cabbages are doing, or dash to help some lame old fellow across the road. In this state, Cecil cannot come anywhere near admitting that he is lonely. Lonely? Rubbish! Look at all these neighbours he knows. In these spells Cecil is understudying for the part of Mr Toad. Oh, and then he cannot understand why they won't let him go on singing in the church choir. "I'm professionally trained as a singer", he will assure you, but be quite deaf to enquiries about when and where.

To label Cecil's problem as loneliness may be to understate it. Clearly his is a clinical condition, and no amount of amateur befriending comes near to meeting his plight. Perhaps we have to say that just as cancer strikes viciously where it will, and there is no rhyme or reason in it (ah, but there is the told-you-so explanation, pointing to tobacco and alcohol), so madness does – and Cecil is unquestionably mad. But then the small voice of commonsense wants to say that surely somewhere along the line Cecil's condition could have been arrested. Surely his present distress was not inevitable.

He started out well enough – caring parents, his older sister with whom he got on well enough (and who has done well for herself), yes, Cecil was off to a good start. He was never particularly clever, but then for most of us that does not matter too much. He was glad to be friendly, only too delighted to do a good turn. Perhaps he could never make close friends, nobody could imagine him married. But he was ever so willing to oblige, with a doggy loyalty to whoever took him up. Those who took him up included employers, but his job record became more and more suspect as he sank from water board clerk, pens in pocket, to warehouse storeman – and he just managed three months there – to airport porter, where he contrived to get invalided out, and claim a disability pension.

In his rare sane moments Cecil is remarkably free from grudge. That is how it goes. But there is bewilderment in it all – did life really mean to deal a precious Cecil such a yarborough, not a court card in sight? It cannot have done, life is not so unfair as that. It must be them – even though they won't admit it. For what Cecil has never been able to admit is his own loneliness. Out of his wild imagination he will summon friends, but somehow they are all busy at the moment. Yes, he talks gladly of his nervous breakdown. That gives him a certain cachet, a badge he can wear with pride like the blood donor's one that is always in his lapel. But to admit that he is in any way responsible for his loneliness, so as to face it, would for him be the final cry of despair, so he lives instead girdled in his world of fantasy. If Mrs So-and-So, and the old man hobbling across the street, let alone those Hogarth bloaters in the pub, all snigger behind his back, then somewhere else there must be somebody who will be only too delighted with his company.

For every Cecil there are thousands of others approaching the borderland of loneliness. Since even psychiatrists often find it hard to reach inside somebody's unhappy mind and grapple with the terror that it hides, those who man the frontiers of social distress look for other causes. A recent report on housing in Salford (September 1986), for instance, lays the blame for so much stress and misery on the high-rise blocks that in the 1960s were rushed up to replace the old terraces. When the lifts break down, the cries of a mother carting her three-year-old up and down a dozen concrete flights speak of her loneliness and despair. A couple of floors above her a bachelor in his mid-twenties is labelled mildly paranoiac, as he fits lock upon lock on his front door. None of them greet one another on the walkways. The pattern of stress and misery is familiar and well-documented.

Housing departments respond by pulling down tower blocks when they can, or at least removing the topmost floors, and when they have the money, instead build low-level high-density housing, much along the ground plans of the nineteenth-century terraces. The hope is that a more natural environment will make it harder for people to feel lonely.

Yet for many years to come, we shall be living with the ruins of the concrete wilderness. Across from Salford in Manchester, the huge housing estate of Hulme, with its twenty-five thousand residents, is a breeding ground for every social problem, not least loneliness. In Victorian times, Hulme was divided and sub-divided into eleven Church of England parishes. Now what was the mother church is used by the African Methodists, and the one Anglican building is a concrete fortress called the Church of the Ascension. It has only high slit windows, covered with wire mesh, and a skylight. To take part in its patronal festival service is to be poignantly aware of the misery of the place. A cheerful congregation responds to the ululations of a black female choir, and the worship is enriched with all the familiar Anglo-Catholic trimmings. A bun-fight follows, and nobody is in a hurry to leave. For outside, in the gloaming of a May evening, lurk the dispossessed youngsters of Hulme, propping up graffiti-smeared walls. A few older residents, still about, edge their way to their own front doors. That act of worship may be a brave celebration of faith in the midst of this despair, but it hardly impinges upon it.

Charles Lowry has left a more romantic picture of life in Manchester, his matchstick figures finding some sort of accommodation to life in the dingy streets and the skyline of factory chimneys. A band marches by, there is a procession, and poverty is tinged with a highlight of hope and togetherness. Manchester is not like that now. *Coronation Street*, after thirty years, trades upon nostalgia. Now the factory chimneys smoke no more, and the wilderness of Hulme and the windy acres of Salford point to a poverty of a different sort. There are no more Manchester wake walks, and only Old Trafford and Maine Road offer rallying points for cheer.

It is a poverty where loneliness stalks. The cramp and cosiness of the Victorian terraces left no room to be lonely. In Manchester now, as elsewhere, while the planners and sociologists work to create more humane housing, charitable bodies pick up some of the pieces. The Selcare Trust is one voluntary organization working in the region to provide those in need with day centres, activity and with somewhere to live. Most of those whom it serves are referred to it by the probation services, such as the dispossessed young men of Hulme.

In 1985 the Carr-Gomm Society opened its first house in Greater Manchester, along the Eccles Road. There was an immediate demand for places in it, and the local committee is seeing whether it can raise money to open more homes locally. Cecil is a potential applicant. In such a setting he could find a measure of self-confidence, and he would have plenty of opportunity to be helpful. It is hard to think how else he might live in the community. The Richmond Fellowship, which specializes in providing halfway homes for people released from mental hospital, might be able to house him for a time, as might MIND, or some similar local voluntary organization. These bodies do not expect to provide permanent homes for people. They offer more professional care, with trained staff, and expect their residents to move on after six months or at most a year. Yet what Cecil needs is somewhere that he can regard as home.

Not every Carr-Gomm resident expects to stay put for ever. Anna is by nature a wanderer. She has been glad enough to stay in a Carr-Gomm house for a couple of years, but now she is getting restless, and cheerfully thinks of moving off again. Others stay, and expect to remain for the rest of their lives. From Carr-Gomm homes there are weddings and funerals, as there are from any other family home. For they set out to be places where lonely people can feel they belong. But then because a house in itself can be isolating, first in Newcastle-upon-Tyne and now in Deptford, the Society runs non-residential workshops where anyone, resident or not, can occupy themselves during the day. It extends the idea of a home beyond four walls and a roof, and is an attempt to ward off loneliness not only during the watches of the night but equally during the long hours of the day.

There are now other organizations in the field. Crossroads

is the name of another nationwide network of voluntary agencies that helps disabled people and those who care for them, by seeing that somebody goes in regularly to do what has to be done for the person in need. For those whom Crossroads supports are people living in their own homes, but unable to look after themselves. They may have a close relative on whose care they depend, but they do need a break from one another sometimes. For total dependency upon another person, or total responsibility for somebody who is disabled, can itself lock two individuals into appalling isolation from one another. They see each other all the time, and there is no respite for either. They are a couple of castaways on a desert island. The familiar routine goes without respite from day to day. They may be swamped with a mutual sense of guilt, one for demanding endless support, the other for giving everything possible, and it is never enough.

Penny and Jack are such a couple. She is confined to a wheelchair, he sells insurance from their home in the depths of the country. She can scarcely ever get away on her own. He has worn out all his goodwill doing what he can to look after her. She envies other women who have been able to abort their marriages and start again on their own. He cannot bear to talk to anybody about himself and the strain from which they suffer, and neighbours prefer to typecast the couple as marvellous. How faithful he is, how patient she is, they say, without enquiring too closely. Yet the couple live only a little below screaming pitch. She can at least write to her friends, and telephone, and so let off steam. He is simply morose.

It is easy for any friend to think of practical suggestions, and a regular visitor whom they both trusted might do much to ease their strain. If Jack knew that there were one morning in the week when he did not have to attend to Penny's needs, if she could look forward to a different pair of helping hands, that might do something to relax the tension. Perhaps they are too proud to call for such help, or to accept it if it were offered. Before her illness they were such good friends, enjoyed books and conversation, but now they have reached a point where she cannot bear his hands touching her, and his efforts grow tense and clumsy. Yet she cannot always manage without him, and looking after her is his mission in life. They are long past being able to talk to one another in any good way, and friends watch impotently from the wings.

Sydney Evans, then Dean of Salisbury Cathedral, in an address on the subject of loneliness (12th October 1980) said: "A wise writer once said that husband and wife should be guardians of each other's solitude. Certainly parents should guard the solitude of their children. For to respect and guard our own solitude is to acknowledge our individual uniqueness and the unique growth we each must achieve. Chosen solitude and chosen prayer enables us really to inhabit the house of our inner self: to know who we are: to know who others are: to know the world in which we are set to live: to know God as the loving Presence in whom we live and move and have our being."

He went on to quote some lines from Vita Sackville-West:

> Book-learning they have known,
> They meet together, talk and grow most wise:
> But they have lost, in losing solitude,
> Something – an inward grace, the seeing eyes,
> The power of being alone:
> The power of being alone with earth and skies,
> Of going about a task with quietude,
> Aware at once of earth's surrounding mood,
> And of an insect crawling on a stone.

Penny and Jack, Cecil, and all the rest of us are afraid to admit that we are lonely because we are afraid of being rejected. At root, we are afraid of ourselves. We are afraid of the towering image of the person that we would like to imagine that we are, well-liked and well-satisfied with what we are making of our lives. That looms over us, mocking our failure. We are even more afraid of the gibbering little self that we dare reveal to nobody, not even ourselves. That poor creature lurks like Mrs Rochester in *Jane Eyre*, shut away in a back room somewhere, and we can hardly bear to unlock the door and give it air. So it is fear that lies underneath all our loneliness, and we are afraid of fear.

"Perfect love", says St John, "casts out fear." In order to be able to love other people, we have to learn to love ourselves. In order to be able to love ourselves, we have to learn to love other people. It is a lifetime's business learning to do both, and to do both at once. Martha and Celia between them reveal the dangers of trying to do one without the other. Martha has always been so interested in herself that, for all her undoubted helpfulness, she is always watching herself in action, and aware of all that she does for others as a veneer. That is how she would like to be seen. Celia is different. She loses herself in all that she does for others, and now that she finds herself widowed confronts a hollow within. There is a conventional misunderstanding of sanctity which would see Celia as altogether excellent, and wonder how in heaven's name she now says that she is lonely. For surely she has done what the Gospel bids, and by losing her life in the service of other people, has found it.

Even that is no proof against loneliness. Jesus kept giving himself for others, yet in Gethsemane and in that bitter word from the cross, "My God, my God, why have you forsaken me?" plumbed the depths of loneliness. There are further hints in the gospels of his loneliness. In those forty days in the wilderness at the start of his ministry, the temptations were to power and manipulation, and he was on his own and lonely in resisting them. In what the gospels describe as his solitary journey into the alien territory of Tyre and Sidon, he went into a house and did not want to be known. There it was only the pestering of a foreign woman that dragged from him what we read as his most reluctant miracle. Yet in his own home town, amongst those who knew him from the past, he was not able to do many miracles. Both abroad and alone, or at home amongst familiar faces, he was impaired. Somewhere in all that lies loneliness, the loneliness that is at the core of our human unhappiness. That Jesus endured it during his lifetime and in the slow hours of his death should be comfort for us all. Loneliness is not a freak condition. It is part of fallen life, and the sooner we admit it the better.

The Perfection of Love
Tony Castle

The great spiritual masters have a message for us today. This is a collection of passages from their writing, drawn from all the traditions of Christianity.

I Am With You
John Woolley

Drawn together by one who works among the seriously ill, this book contains prayers which will bring comfort and help to the troubled.

Moments With God
Georgette Butcher

A collection of prayers and readings specially designed for women. The author shows how God can help and guide us through the changing pattern of each day.

Yes, Lord, I Believe
Dom Edmund Jones

". . . a very positive and practical book . . . a helpful source of prayer. The freshness, honesty and vitality of its style ensure that its message is deeply and immediately felt."
The Universe

Gateway to God
Simone Weil

"Simone . . . makes everything seem, at once, reassuringly recognizable and so luminous as to be heavenly . . . the great mysteries . . . are seen through a window of time in the perspective of eternity."

Malcolm Muggeridge

Waiting on God
Simone Weil

"The best spiritual writer of this century."

André Gide

The Divine Pity
Gerald Vann

"Gerald Vann . . . offers us a vision by which people can . . . be stimulated to make new and intelligent attempts to act lovingly in the world."

From the Foreword by Simon Tugwell

An Approach to Christianity
Bishop Christopher Butler

". . . an impressive piece of apologetic . . . With its insistence on man's capacity to think, and on his need to make free and responsible decisions, it speaks from an old tradition of Christian humanism which demands our respect."

Church Times

I Believe
Trevor Huddleston

A simple, prayerful series of reflections on the phrases of the Creed. This is a beautiful testament of the strong, quiet inner faith of a man best known for his active role in the Church – and in the world.

The Heart of the Christian Faith
Donald Coggan

The author ". . . presents the essential core of Christianity in a marvellously simple and readable form, quite uncluttered by any excess of theological technicality."

The Yorkshire Post

Be Still and Know
Michael Ramsey

The former Archbishop of Canterbury looks at prayer in the New Testament, at what the early mystics could teach us about it, and at some practical aspects of Christian praying.

Pilgrim's Progress
John Bunyan

"A masterpiece which generation after generation of ordinary men and women have taken to their hearts."

Hugh Ross Williamson

Half Way
Jim Thompson

We all have to face the changes that middle age brings. Jim Thompson shows how this can be a time of growth, development and change for the better in all areas of our life.

". . . a warm, stimulating book . . ."
John King, Church of England Newspaper

Now and For Ever
Anne Townsend

"A well-researched, highly relevant book on all aspects of marriage today . . . Amidst the current spate of books on marriage, this one stands apart, deserving a place on the best sellers list."
Susan Rimmer, Church of England Newspaper

Mother Teresa: Contemplative in the Heart of the World
Angelo Devananda

This book focuses upon the spirituality which has inspired the wonderful work of Mother Teresa among the poor and dying, consisting mainly of long passages of her own words.

Fount Paperbacks

Fount is one of the leading paperback publishers of religious books and below are some of its recent titles.

- ☐ THE WAY OF THE CROSS Richard Holloway £1.95
- ☐ LIKE WIND ON THE GRASSES Rita Snowden £1.95
- ☐ AN INTRODUCTION TO MARITAL PROBLEMS Jack Dominian £2.50
- ☐ I AM WITH YOU John Woolley £2.95
- ☐ NOW AND FOR EVER Anne Townsend £1.95
- ☐ THE PERFECTION OF LOVE Tony Castle £2.95
- ☐ A PROPHETIC PEOPLE Clifford Hill £2.95
- ☑ THOMAS MORE Richard Marius £7.95
- ☐ WALKING IN THE LIGHT David Winter £1.95
- ☐ HALF WAY Jim Thompson £2.50
- ☐ THE HEART OF THE BIBLE George Appleton £4.95
- ☐ I BELIEVE Trevor Huddleston £1.75
- ☐ PRESENT CONCERNS C. S. Lewis £1.95
- ☐ PSALMS OF PRAISE Frances Hogan £2.50
- ☐ MOTHER TERESA: CONTEMPLATIVE IN THE HEART OF THE WORLD Angelo Devananda £2.50
- ☐ IN THE HURRICANE Adrian Hastings £2.50

All Fount paperbacks are available at your bookshop or newsagent, or they can be ordered by post from Fount Paperbacks, Cash Sales Department, G.P.O. Box 29, Douglas, Isle of Man. Please send purchase price plus 22p per book, maximum postage £3. Customers outside the UK send purchase price, plus 22p per book. Cheque, postal order or money order. No currency.

NAME (Block letters) _____

ADDRESS_____

_____

_____

While every effort is made to keep prices low, it is sometimes necessary to increase them at short notice. Fontana Paperbacks reserve the right to show new retail prices on covers which may differ from those previously advertised in the text or elsewhere.